3D Printing for Architects with MakerBot

Build state-of-the-art architecture design projects with MakerBot Replicator 1, 2, or 2X

Matthew B. Stokes

PUBLISHING

BIRMINGHAM - MUMBAI

3D Printing for Architects with MakerBot

First published: November 2013

Production Reference: 1141113

Published by Packt Publishing Ltd.
Livery Place
35 Livery Street
Birmingham B3 2PB, UK.

ISBN 978-1-78355-075-3

www.packtpub.com

Cover Image by Suresh Mogre (suresh.mogre.99@gmail.com)

Credits

Author
Matthew B. Stokes

Reviewers
Dong-Joo Kim
Andrew Plumb

Acquisition Editors
Aarthi Kumaraswamy
Kevin Colaco

Commissioning Editors
Neha Nagwekar
Sharvari Tawde

Technical Editor
Amit Ramadas

Project Coordinator
Sageer Parkar

Proofreader
Clyde Jenkins

Indexer
Priya Subramani

Production Coordinator
Shantanu Zagade

Cover Work
Shantanu Zagade

About the Author

Matthew B. Stokes graduated with a combined Mechanical Engineering and Computer Science Dual Degree and Technological Entrepreneurship Certificate from the University of Western Ontario. He is interested and has been actively involved in consumer 3D printing since 2009, and has completed an Engineering Co-op at KnowRoaming—a Canada-based technology company, where he worked to design and test 3D-printed cellphone cases for embedding hardware. He has owned and operated a MakerBot Replicator since spring 2012, and has competed in several 3D printing design contests.

Currently, Matthew is back at the University of Western Ontario completing a Master's degree in Biomedical Engineering in a collaboration model involving Muscular Skeletal Health Research (CMHR) and Computer Aided Medical Intervention (CAMI) under Dr. Louis Ferreira. His expected date of graduation is 2015.

Matthew has a wide range of interests outside 3D printing, including Raspberry Pi, Android applications, hackathons, Tough Mudder events, and design challenges.

I'd like to thank my parents for being so supportive, my good friend Sean Watson for continually fueling my interest in 3D printing, and my girlfriend Meghan Piccinin for helping push me to complete this book.

About the Reviewers

Dong-Joo Kim is an architectural designer, LEED AP currently living and practicing in New York City.

She completed her Bachelor of Architecture degree from Pratt Institute, Brooklyn, in 2009 and has worked as a designer and 3D visualization instructor in several countries around the world, including Singapore and Germany. She also received her McNeel Rhinoceros Level I authorized trainer certification in 2011 from Malaysia.

Having her academic background and professional experience in the United States, Europe, and Asia, she has a broad, yet keen perspective in design, planning, and ideas. Her multidisciplinary training and exposure to cultural diversities aid her continually evolve into an adaptive thinker as well as a fearless explorer.

She enjoys venturing and experimenting with new technologies as a means to develop her designs and communicate with the world. Her most recent obsession is playing with MakerBot, day and night, and she believes it is a valuable tool that brings a whole new level of clarity and precision in the design process.

To view her academic and professional design work, please visit www.dongjookim.com.

Andrew Plumb is, by day, an Electrical Engineer specializing in Electronic Design Automation (EDA) software and design flows for integrated circuit (IC) design. By night and on weekends, expanding the frontiers of open source 3D printing hardware and software keep him occupied.

> My thanks to Adrian Bowyer for establishing the RepRap project, and to the extended Open Source Hardware community for all of your contributions. Machines like these wouldn't exist for the rest of us without your efforts.

www.packtpub.com

Support files, eBooks, discount offers and more

You might want to visit www.PacktPub.com for support files and downloads related to your book.

Did you know that Packt offers eBook versions of every book published, with PDF and ePub files available? You can upgrade to the eBook version at www.PacktPub.com and as a print book customer, you are entitled to a discount on the eBook copy. Get in touch with us at service@packtpub.com for more details.

At www.PacktPub.com, you can also read a collection of free technical articles, sign up for a range of free newsletters and receive exclusive discounts and offers on Packt books and eBooks.

http://PacktLib.PacktPub.com

Do you need instant solutions to your IT questions? PacktLib is Packt's online digital book library. Here, you can access, read and search across Packt's entire library of books.

Why Subscribe?

- Fully searchable across every book published by Packt
- Copy and paste, print and bookmark content
- On demand and accessible via web browser

Free Access for Packt account holders

If you have an account with Packt at www.PacktPub.com, you can use this to access PacktLib today and view nine entirely free books. Simply use your login credentials for immediate access.

Table of Contents

Table of Contents

Preface

Welcome to *3D Printing for Architects with MakerBot*! This book will take you through the process of building 3D prototypes for simple to cutting-edge architectural design projects using MakerBot Replicator (1, 2, or 2X) and other allied software packages.

What this book covers

Chapter 1, A Primer on 3D Printing, introduces you to different methodologies, technologies, materials, and history of 3D printing with a focus on the MakerBot Replicator 2X.

Chapter 2, 3D Modeling Software, introduces you to modeling practices useful in 3D printing with common free and paid 3D modeling software.

Chapter 3, 3D Printing Software, covers the topic of transforming a 3D model into a 3D print.

Chapter 4, Multicolor Design, explains the utilization of the multiple heads on the MakerBot Replicator 2 in the design process for a model composed of two distinctly different colors.

Chapter 5, Multipart Design, introduces you to creating more advanced assemblies. A special focus is on component tolerance.

Chapter 6, The Community – Thingiverse and GrabCAD, helps you in finding and modifying online CAD resources into an existing design. It also shows how valuable and powerful the community around MakerBot is.

Chapter 7, Iterative Design, explains a culminating example of several iterations of an apartment building's floor plan.

What you need for this book

You will require the following for this book:

- Must own a MakerBot Replicator 1, 2, or 2X
- Must have basic conceptual understanding of architectural design/ engineering drawing such as perspectives and ratios and proportions

Who this book is for

This book is for architects who want to gain an unfair advantage over their competitors during their client pitches, by wowing the clients with their sophisticated yet cost-effective 3D design prototypes and faster delivery time through the incorporation of 3D printing into their architectural design workflow.

Conventions

In this book, you will find a number of styles of text that distinguish between different kinds of information. Here are some examples of these styles, and an explanation of their meaning.

Code words in text are shown as follows: " The files `ch5_clearance_guide_holes.stl` and `ch5_clearance_guide_shaft.stl` are extremely useful."

New terms and **important words** are shown in bold. Words that you see on the screen, in menus or dialog boxes for example, appear in the text like this: "Click on **Make** located at the top of the screen to open up the print options."

When mentioned if staring at an object from the front, the X axis refers to the left and right directions, the Y axis refers to the towards and away directions, and the Z axis refers to the above or below directions.

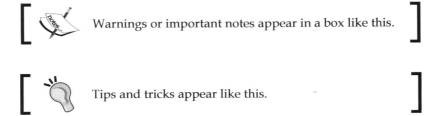

Warnings or important notes appear in a box like this.

Tips and tricks appear like this.

Reader feedback

Feedback from our readers is always welcome. Let us know what you think about this book—what you liked or may have disliked. Reader feedback is important for us to develop titles that you really get the most out of.

To send us general feedback, simply send an e-mail to feedback@packtpub.com, and mention the book title via the subject of your message.

If there is a topic that you have expertise in and you are interested in either writing or contributing to a book, see our author guide on www.packtpub.com/authors.

Customer support

Now that you are the proud owner of a Packt book, we have a number of things to help you to get the most from your purchase.

Downloading the example code

You can download the example code files for all Packt books you have purchased from your account at http://www.packtpub.com. If you purchased this book elsewhere, you can visit http://www.packtpub.com/support and register to have the files e-mailed directly to you.

Errata

Although we have taken every care to ensure the accuracy of our content, mistakes do happen. If you find a mistake in one of our books—maybe a mistake in the text or the code—we would be grateful if you would report this to us. By doing so, you can save other readers from frustration and help us improve subsequent versions of this book. If you find any errata, please report them by visiting http://www.packtpub.com/submit-errata, selecting your book, clicking on the **errata submission form** link, and entering the details of your errata. Once your errata are verified, your submission will be accepted and the errata will be uploaded on our website, or added to any list of existing errata, under the Errata section of that title. Any existing errata can be viewed by selecting your title from http://www.packtpub.com/support.

Piracy

Piracy of copyright material on the Internet is an ongoing problem across all media. At Packt, we take the protection of our copyright and licenses very seriously. If you come across any illegal copies of our works, in any form, on the Internet, please provide us with the location address or website name immediately so that we can pursue a remedy.

Please contact us at copyright@packtpub.com with a link to the suspected pirated material.

We appreciate your help in protecting our authors, and our ability to bring you valuable content.

Questions

You can contact us at questions@packtpub.com if you are having a problem with any aspect of the book, and we will do our best to address it.

1
A Primer on 3D Printing

With the growing demand and increasing applications of 3D printing, it is important that we take a look at the history and some basic concepts before jumping on to the actual working of MakerBots. We will begin by covering a brief history on 3D printing, including a description of some of the main methods and technologies currently in use. Next, we will familiarize ourselves with the MakerBot, covering a select few of its specifications and the impact these have on printed parts. Lastly, we will touch on printing limitations using the MakerBot and the different material options available for use.

A brief history of 3D printing

Over the last several years, we have seen a tremendous increase in media attention surrounding 3D printing, as new technical advancements have led the number of applications to grow exponentially and encompass a broad range of disciplines. Today, 3D printing is being used across a plethora of industries, in applications that are pushing the limits of modern technology and innovation. While the new printing technology is revolutionary, 3D printing itself has been around for almost 30 years, beginning in 1984 with Charles Hull, who later went on to co-found 3D Systems in 1986. By modifying technology used in traditional two-dimensional inkjet printers, Hull created the first 3D printer, patenting the method of **stereolithography** (**SLA**) and introduced the industry to additive manufacturing.

Understanding stereolithography

In SLA printing, an ultraviolet laser traces the cross-section of a part onto the surface of a vat containing an ultraviolet curable photopolymer resin. The resin exposed to the light will cure and solidify, sticking to the layer below it before the platform descends by a set distance and more liquid resin is added to the vat. This process will repeat for each subsequent cross-sectional layer until the three-dimensional part has been created. The following image illustrates this process:

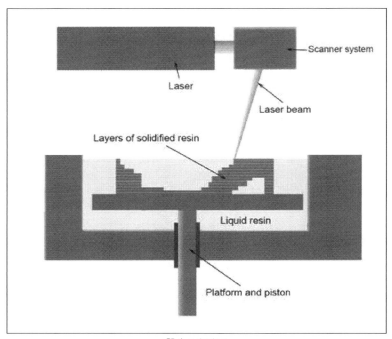

SLA printing

The source of this image can be found at http://en.wikipedia.org/wiki/ File:Stereolithography_apparatus.jpg#filelinks.

Downloading the example code

You can download the example code files for all Packt books you have purchased from your account at http://www.packtpub.com. If you purchased this book elsewhere, you can visit http://www.packtpub. com/support and register to have the files e-mailed directly to you.

SLA printing began the additive manufacturing revolution and remained the main 3D printing process until mid-1980 when Dr. Carl Deckand and Dr. Joseph Beaman, with sponsorship from DARPA, developed and patented **Selective Laser Sintering (SLS)**.

Learning about Selective Laser Sintering

SLS fuses small particles of material (plastic, metal, ceramic, or glass) using a high- powered laser. The technique is similar to SLA printing in such a way that the laser traces the cross-sectional shape before a platform descends. Perhaps the biggest advantage of SLS printing is that the granular material supports the top layer of material, giving rise to part geometry not previously possible using SLA printing without some sort of supporting structure created underneath the model.

An example of this is illustrated in the following image in the printing of one side of an inverted two-dimensional triangle. If the internal angle of the pyramid is low, there is enough material in the bottom layer for the current layer to sit on top (**B**). However, by increasing the angle, we eventually reach a point where none of our current layer is sitting on top of the bottom layer, but rather is floating in space as seen in **A** in the following image:

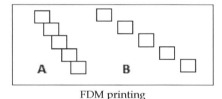

FDM printing

In SLS printing, the top layer will sit on unsintered powder, whereas with SLA printing, the layer will fall to the platform, ruining the print.

It took a number of years before an SLS printer came to the market, in which time S. Scott Crump invented, patented, and brought to the market **Fused Deposition Modeling (FDM)** and later went on to co-found Stratasys.

Basics of Fused Deposition Modeling

In FDM, the material is fed from a spool through an extrusion nozzle where either the nozzle or the platform is moving, so as to again trace the cross-section of the desired part at the given layer onto the platform. The nozzle has control to turn the flow on/off and in general applications, the nozzle is heated to melt a thermoplastic material, which immediately hardens, solidifying to the layer below it. This process can be seen in the following image:

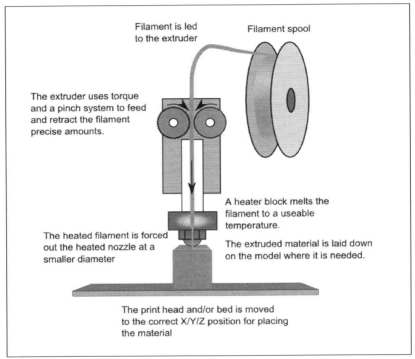

Filament is led to the extruder

Filament spool

The extruder uses torque and a pinch system to feed and retract the filament precise amounts.

A heater block melts the filament to a useable temperature.

The heated filament is forced out the heated nozzle at a smaller diameter

The extruded material is laid down on the model where it is needed.

The print head and/or bed is moved to the correct X/Y/Z position for placing the material

FDM printing

The source of this image can be found at `http://reprap.org/wiki/File:FFF.png`.

Similar to SLA printing, FDM requires a supporting structure to account for layers *floating in space*. FDM printing is the technique used by the vast majority of the open-source and consumer ($300-$5,000) 3D printers. The major advantage of this technique is the cost of material as FDM printing most commonly uses ABS thermoplastic, which costs fractions of pennies per gram. MakerBot is one such example of an FDM-based printer.

The origin of MakerBot

The RepRap project was founded in 2005 by Dr. Adrian Bowyer, who can be credited for being the first to target the hobbyist/DIY/early adopter community. The intended purpose of the RepRap project was to be an open source, affordable, self-replicating 3D printer (self-replicating meaning capable of producing all its own parts with the exception of electrical components). All of RepRap's printer specifications are released to the open source community who contribute to its evolution. MakerBot would later be birthed in 2009 from progress made by RepRap printers.

MakerBot's first printer was the CupCake CNC in early 2009, which was a **repstrap** (3D printer cobbled together from whatever parts you can find, which will eventually allow you to print the parts for a RepRap machine, or to simply use as a standalone machine). After the CupCake came the Thing-O-Matic in late 2010, followed by the Replicator in early 2012, and ending with the Replicator 2 and 2X (eXtreme), released late 2012. Between each release, monumental changes were made, as the technology was evolving in leaps and bounds. The CupCake and Thing-O-Matic printers were DIY kits by default, whereas the Replicators, by default, came preassembled. Probably, the biggest source of controversy in MakerBot's history was the announcement that the Replicator 2 would be a closed source project. While this shocked the loyal MakerBot community, MakerBot did not slow down and on June 19, 2013, they were acquired by Stratasys for $403 million USD.

 FDM is a trademarked term by Stratasys. Members of the open source community coined an equivalent term Fused Filament Fabrication in order to use a term that is unconstrained.

Applications of 3D printing

From examination of SLA, SLS, and FDM, we can generalize the concept of 3D printing to be an additive manufacturing process that takes a digital model, slices the model into layers, attaches material onto a platform following the cross-section of the model, and lastly, drops the platform, repeating the process of laying material until the 3D model has been recreated.

The first commercial 3D printers were intended for use in rapid prototyping. By incorporating 3D printing into the design life cycle, engineers could reduce both time and cost between product revisions. SLA, SLS, and FDM can be considered the base models for more highly specialized printers that have developed since the 1990s, including **Direct Metal Deposition (DMD)**, **Direct Metal Laser Sintering (DMLS)**, **Electron Beam Melting (EBM) Laser Consolidation (LC)**, and **Multi-Jet Modeling (MJM)**.

Product design

By providing a rapid and inexpensive solution, 3D printing is perhaps most useful in any application that requires iterative development. A company may go through several stages of iterative development before finally arriving at a final product with each stage being a slight modification of the last. These customized modifications are something that can now be offered to the consumer. You are capable of not only downloading a model for say a lamp, but you are also able to personalize your lamp (for example, adjust the height and curvature) before purchase or download to print on your own printer.

Healthcare

Around the late 1990s, we began to see 3D printing being explored for the first time in medical applications and in the early 2000s, researchers at the Wake Forest Institute for Regenerative Medicine successfully printed a miniature functional kidney able to filter blood and produce urine in animal testing. This would be the first major successful application of 3D printing in medicine, but in the coming years, we would see advancements in 3D printed patient-specific prosthetics, surgical implants, cells, blood vessels, organs, casts, biomaterials, and many other medical uses. Perhaps the most fascinating aspect of 3D bioprinting is its patient-specific application. That, by using CT scans or other means doctors can tailor a completely customized solution specific to a patient's exact needs.

Food

One of the most recent largely mediatized applications for 3D printing is food. On June 14, 2013, NASA awarded a $125,000 contract to build a 3D printer that can make pizzas. In the past, there have been other food projects, including chocolate, pasta, cookies, sugar structures, and 3D printed meats (however, with a price tag of over $300,000 USD, 3D printed meats are far from a viable food source...yet).

Fashion

While companies such as Nike have traditionally used 3D printing in their engineering design iterations, today 3D printing in fashion has exploded. Companies are emerging that are 3D-printing custom fit shoes, high heels, jewelry, sun glasses, accessories, and even clothing. With the immergence of new 3D printing material mediums, the fashion industry can design for style, function, and comfort.

Additional applications

The applications for 3D printing are ever-expanding as new companies push the boundaries of current technology. We are 3D-printing structures impossible to ever duplicate using modern manufacturing, as we push the envelope of efficiency. 3D-printed clothing, shoes, accessories, and jewelry allow us to truly express our individuality, while 3D-printed guns call into question current laws and regulations. 3D-printed musical instruments allow us to create new musical dynamics, and 3D printing on the nanoscale is opening doors to new stronger, lighter materials.

MakerBot Replicator 2X specifications

The following image shows the MakerBot Replicator 2 printing specifications. These specifications are identical to the Replicator 2X except for build volume, which in 2X has decreased to 9.7 L x 6.0 W x 6.1 H due to a second print head being added.

PRINTING		
Print Technology:	Fused Filament Fabrication	
Build Volume:	11.2 L x 6.0 W x 6.1 H in [28.5 x 15.3 x 15.5 cm]	
Layer Resolution Settings:	High	100 microns [0.0039 in]
	Standard	200 microns [0.0078 in]
	Low	300 microns [0.0118 in]
Positioning Precision:	XY: 11 microns [0.0004 in]; Z: 2.5 microns [0.0001 in]	
Filament Diameter:	1.75 mm [0.069 in]	
Nozzle Diameter:	0.4 mm [0.015 in]	

MakerBot Replicator 2 print specifications

Printing with MakerBot

Build volume is self-explanatory, but what's important to note are the maximum dimensions in each of the axes, as these will limit the part size and constrain orientation.

Before printing, we will have the opportunity to specify the intended part resolution—the higher the resolution, the longer the print duration.

 It is recommended to only use high resolution when absolutely necessary or for small parts, as print times are approximately doubled from a medium and tripled from a low resolution print.

The most important specification to note is the XY precision (11 microns) and Z precision (2.5 microns). These are absolute limits which must be considered during part design. Also, note how Z precision is over 4x that of XY. For the majority of applications, this will not make a difference; however, if you are desperately seeking a little more precision, this is a fact that can be exploited.

MakerBot Replicators uses a 1.75 mm filament. It will not accept a 3.00 mm filament and often times cheaper 1.75 mm filament will in actuality be closer to 2.00 mm and jam the extruder.

MakerBot Replicator 2X limitations

MakerBot is considered the leader in consumer 3D printers; however, FDM/FFF technology still faces many limitations, including stepping, precision, time, and supports.

Stepping

Physical steps between layers are caused by having to slice the model and use a 2D cross section to print each layer. Stepping on curved surfaces is the most noticeable feature, but this will also occur on any surface where, looking normal to the z-axis, we see an angular increase or decrease in the cross section. In general, lower precision will cause more prominent steps between layers, but can reduce print time, freeing up machines, and increasing throughput. Stepping can been seen in the following image:

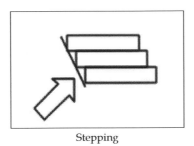

Stepping

Precision

Precision is largely the difference between a 3D printer that costs thousands of dollars and a printer that costs hundreds of thousands of dollars. The Replicator 2X has the best precision of any previous printer made by MakerBot, but we need to keep in mind its limitations.

As a rule of thumb, we will require a minimum of 2 layers to form a wall, as any less than this has the tendency to produce unexpected results.

Time

The first person/company to create a 3D printer that prints similarly to injection molding will become extraordinarily wealthy; currently, time is not our ally. It would take a couple of days to print a solid cube that fills the entire MakerBot build volume. Size, precision, and infill will all add time to a print. Fortunately, we have control over these print settings.

Supports

As mentioned earlier, supports are required to support sharp overhangs. The supports are printed differently so that when the part is finished, they can simply be broken away. However, there may be some remnants, which a little bit of sanding or a utility knife can easily remove.

MakerBot Replicator 2X material options

MakerBot Replicator 2 can only print in PLA. The Replicator 2X has a wide range of materials for printing, including ABS, PLA, PVA, and Nylon; however, we are going to focus on the two most common plastics: ABS and PLA. Additionally, Replicator 2X has two heads which can be loaded with two different materials.

ABS

If you have ever played with LEGO or have taken a look at the pipes under your sink, you've come across ABS. ABS has high impact resistance, is tough and resilient, and costs fractions of pennies per gram. This material has been used in nearly all FFF applications up until the recent adoption of PLA.

The drawback to ABS is curling upon cooling, which can pose big problems for larger objects. Curling can cause large flat objects to "banana boat" up, where the corners will curl as the materials cools. MakerBot has addressed this problem by adding a heated build platform and enclosing the sides, keeping the build volume warm to avoid cooling until the print is completed. These measures have helped substantially, though the problem still exists.

The amount of curling is largely dependent on the geometry of the part, and it will vary on a case-by-case basis.

PLA

PLA has similar properties to ABS but with the distinct advantage of minimal shrinking while cooling. This property is fundamental, as we no longer require a heated build platform or maintenance of a higher constant temperature while cooling, saving up to 32 percent on electricity use.

This book will be using PLA as the material choice for all examples, which will begin in the next chapter.

Summary

In this chapter, we have covered a brief history of 3D printing, including a generalized introduction to the different processes of 3D printing. We covered the birth of MakerBot and learned about the wide usability of 3D printing in everything from medicine to food. Next, we learned about our MakerBot Replicators' specifications, and we touched on some of the limitations that these impose. We ended by talking about the most common material choices, leading into the next chapter, where we will learn briefly about solid modeling and designing to print on the MakerBot Replicator.

2
3D Modeling Software

This chapter will discuss the most common 3D modeling software, including both free and paid. We will be introduced to some basic solid modeling concepts and best practices for creating models intended to print on the MakerBot Replicator 2X. This chapter will end with a practical example converting a 2D architectural drawing of a roof truss into a 3D model, and saved to a format capable of being imported into 3D printing software. We cover the following topics in this chapter:

- Modeling software comparison
- General modeling theory
- An example of a roof truss

Modeling software comparison

There are hundreds of **Computer Aided Design** (**CAD**) software options available; the challenge aspect is finding the one that works for your specific needs. The price of a software package can range from free to tens of thousands of dollars, but the price does not necessarily make one package better than another. We will be covering some of the most common packages, but I invite you to check out `http://en.wikipedia.org/wiki/Category:Computer-aided_design_software` for a comprehensive list of available CAD options.

We will categorize CAD packages into three distinct groups: beginner, intermediate, and advanced. The difference between categories is based on the available features useful for modeling and the initial learning curve. Note that many of the more advanced CAD packages come with tools useful in animation, simulation, dynamic analysis, and rendering. We are focused on modeling but if you wish to learn more about any of these additional tools, you should check out the package's respective website for more information.

Be aware of licensing restrictions for each software package. A personal use or educational package is often offered with paid software; however, within the terms and conditions, it usually states works produced using this license may not be used for commercial or monetary purposes.

Using beginner software packages

Beginner software packages are a great place to get started if you have little to no experience working within a 3D environment. They will introduce you to some basic elements of 3D modeling and allow you to begin creating simple, shaped parts. Once you get an understanding and start becoming comfortable with the idea of 3D modeling, I recommend you to check out an intermediate or advanced package to give you the ability to create more advanced models and to have a little more control over the details of your model.

TinkerCAD

TinkerCAD offers a completely free package that will get you up and started. However, if you intend to use the software for any sort of commercial purposes, you must purchase a license. The license, which compared to many of the other packages we are going to mention, is offered on a month-by-month basis at an extremely affordable price of $19 USD/month.

TinkerCAD is a browser-based 3D design platform that works on the basis of dragging-and-dropping preset shapes onto a work plane. These shapes can be combined and their dimensions manipulated to form parts.

Autodesk123D

Autodesk123D has a free package that offers limited Cloud storage capabilities, and a premium package (at approximately $10/month) offering additional access to models and extra storage space. Similar to TinkerCAD, Autodesk123D has a browser-based 3D design platform; however, it differs substantially by not binding the user into using premade 3D shapes, but rather allowing for the creation the user's own shapes derived from sketches. Autodesk123D is also available for the desktops, iOS, and Android platforms.

Using intermediate software packages

The packages in this category give us more explicit control over our design, particularly in creating parametric models. Parametric modeling allows us to go back to our model's history and change parameters that we have previously set, allowing us to fine-tune features. Some of these packages also come packed with additional options and features, and can include software add-ons with animation, rendering, documentation, or other useful features.

FreeCAD

FreeCAD is a personal favorite, as it is an open source, free package that can be used on Windows, Mac OS X, and Linux.

FreeCAD has a helpful community with plenty of tutorials to get you up and running with their comprehensive assortment of modeling features.

Autodesk 3DS Max

Autodesk 3DS Max is considered a quintessential 3D architectural design and the favorite of most architects. This package, with its powerful rendering engine, is capable of creating static or animated models that can look like real photographs. With a price tag of just over $3,500 USD, it should be a serious consideration if you are looking for professional models, graphics, and animations. Additionally, being part of the Autodesk family, this software is capable of interoperating with many of their other products.

Autodesk AutoCAD and SolidWorks

AutoCAD and SolidWorks are complete engineering/architectural design software packages also utilizing parametric design. Both have a starting price upwards of $4,000 for commercial use.

These packages are recommended once you have a more solid understanding of 3D modeling and are looking to create more complex parametric models. Both of these packages are filled with additional features and tools useful in the design process, including rendering, animation, and many validation tools and add-ons.

Rhinoceros

Rhino is a favorite of many designers and architects because of its low cost and extensive feature list. At a cost of about $1,000 USD, this software package has many of the high-end design and rendering features found inside AutoCAD and SolidWorks at a price that won't empty your wallet.

Using advanced software packages

These packages have a steep initial learning curve, as they are packed full of useful tools for modeling. All the tools may seem a little overwhelming at first, but they give you absolute control and speed in creating incredibly detailed models once you have some practice using them. These packages also come with impressive rendering engines capable of producing beautiful images and animations for your models.

Blender

Blender is perhaps one of the most impressive open source, free software packages for 3D modeling, rendering, and animation. Blender is capable of producing movie-quality graphics and animations, and gives you absolute control in creation. There is a steep learning curve while first using this software, but the possibilities are truly endless.

The beautiful thing about open source software is the community that works together to constantly build, improve, and refine. In Blender, you will find an extraordinary amount of plugins and if there is not one readily available with a little searching, you can most likely find one in development or beta. If you want to be really bold, you can also design one yourself. With that being said, there are plugins to help assist in preparing Blender models to 3D print.

Regardless of which software you choose, there will be a learning curve at the beginning. However, once you hold your first model in your hands, it'll make it all worthwhile. Going forward, the CAD package we have chosen for all examples is SolidWorks.

General modeling theory

Modeling allows for both additive and subtractive design practices. The purpose of our model needs to be taken into consideration before we start designing, as we have two distinctly different design methodologies we can utilize.

First, we can follow very strict and exact modeling, which is often the case when we are doing any product design or iterative work. This methodology is the most common, and occurs when we add dimensions to our models. This is known as **Solid Modeling** or **Parametric Modeling**. The second is more of an artist approach to modeling in which we model akin to shaping a piece of clay. This approach is most common while designing parts that have many free-flowing curved surfaces, such as the body of a car. This is known as **Freeform Surface Modeling**.

For our purposes, we will be utilizing the first approach, Solid Modeling, as this more closely relates to our architectural design applications.

Design practices

We touched on a few design practices briefly in *Chapter 1, A Primer on 3D Printing*, in the *MakerBot Replicator 2X limitations* section, which we will now expand upon by using examples for several different design scenarios. What's most important is to consider that the printer functions by taking a 3D model, slicing it into *n* number of 2D layers, and applying material in areas specified by the cross-section. Keeping this in mind, we can see how some of the scenarios outlined in this section will produce unpredictable results.

Objects must be closed

3D printing requires that our object be a solid or has a volume rather than a surface. Surfaces are used inside CAD packages to create more complex shapes and add more control to model faces. Surfaces have the property of 0 thickness, and when we are ready to print, they must be explicitly given a thickness. The model must be watertight; think "creating volumes". Open objects are considered to be non-manifold.

Objects must be manifold

For our purposes, an object will become nonmanifold if one of its edges or vertices is shared between two or more faces, as depicted in the following image figure, and also if it is not closed as previously described:

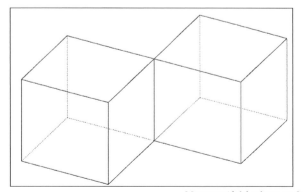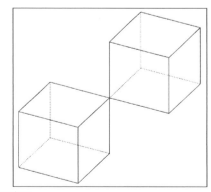

Nonmanifold edges and vertices

This is a very poor modeling practice and should be avoided at all cost, as it produces undesired and unpredictable results in both 3D printing and any simulation studies. The solution is to either connect the two bodies or create two entirely separate parts.

There are a number of websites and software packages available to help you fix questionable meshes. If you require more intensive mesh refinement features, you will most likely be looking at a paid software solution; however, for general fixing purposes, netfabb Basic is a free program worth checking out.

 For more information on manifold conditions or common errors with nonmanifold objects, check out the link `http://www.shapeways.com/tutorials/fixing-non-manifold-models`.

Maintain a minimum wall thickness

This is a point that often gets overlooked. From experience, I recommend not going under 0.4 mm wall thickness in XY (0.4 mm is the thickness of the extruder nozzle) and 0.2 mm in Z (2 shells of the minimal layer height 0.1 mm). Going under this wall thickness most commonly produces small voids of material in the wall and other unpredictable errors. Walls below this thickness are also extremely flexible and break easily.

While the XY minimal wall thickness is fixed by the extruder nozzle diameter, the Z thickness is changeable. If our model contains a Z section that has a thickness of 0.2 mm, this can be achieved using the high (0.1 mm) layer resolution settings (more on this in *Chapter 3, 3D Printing Software*). Using a low (0.3 mm) layer resolution in this circumstance will result in unpredictable results. Therefore, the highest bound of your parts layer resolution settings will be dictated by the minimum layer resolution you expect to resolve.

Orientation considerations

Depending on the shape's geometry, some orientations will produce better, more accurate results. Consider trying to print a triangular wedge. If we orient the print upright (depth in XY), the last several layers leading to the point will be very fragile, whereas if we orient the print flat (depth in Z), we will produce smooth crisp corners.

Size and precision

Our model must fit inside the build volume. If it doesn't, there are several design changes that are left for us to debate as follows:

- **Scale**: Scaling will shrink every dimension of the model by the scale factor value. If you have any absolute values in your model (for example, a 1 mm screw hole), consider another option as this scales *all* the dimensions.

- **Create multiple parts**: Super glue is your best friend while working with the MakerBot, as it actually fuses ABS or PLA. Cut your model into two sections, print each section separately, and then super glue the pieces together. You can also add connection features (for example, slot and peg) to help align two parts together.

This technique of splitting and gluing is also often useful for parts where some components require greater accuracy or different orientations to improve quality. Rather than printing the entire model with high accuracy, you can make the high accuracy piece/section as its own model and simply glue it onto the base, which can save hours of print time.

- **Redesign**: Sometimes you have no other option than to go back to the drawing board.

Text

Font font font! Make it easy on yourself and your MakerBot by choosing a font whose characters are all in caps and have minimal curvature.

Example – roof truss

Let's go through a practical example of modeling and create a roof truss. We begin by sketching or finding an image of what we would like to model. We'll use the illustration below:

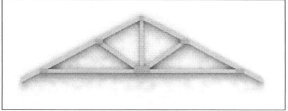

Common roof truss

Preparation of drawing for modeling

Now we are faced with our first design decision: create the part with real dimensions and scale it for 3D printing or use prescaled dimensions to fit on the MakerBot platform. What you choose will depend on your application. The quickest way, if you already know you intend to print the model on the MakerBot, is to design for printing from the start. The disadvantage of this decision is that you are sacrificing some accuracy in the model, as you are designing to the MakerBots platform specifications; however, this only becomes important if you are doing quantitative testing or product development, whereas our application is more so a visual model. For this example, we will be designing to optimize for printing on our MakerBot from the beginning.

Let's consider a size for this model. For the purposes of simplicity, we'll have our entire model fit easily in the build platform. Thus, let's set a size of approximately half the build platform width for the bottom joist. Alternatively, we could have also chosen to model the truss as an assembly (grouping of several components) and put together all the parts after printing. Both options are valid.

Our last step before getting into the detailed design is to look for any problem areas that might arise. Looking at our original image seen previously, we notice the gussets. We must ensure that the XY-thickness of these gussets is above our absolute minimal wall thickness of 0.4 mm and the Z-thickness is above 0.1 mm (though we should aim for minimum of 2 walls thick). This appears to be the only area of concern, so now we can begin designing.

Ensure that the units you are using in CAD are the same units you intend to print with. For example, if you are designing in mm, ensure that your part fits within the mm platform size and maximal height.

Designing the roof truss

The CAD package we have chosen is SolidWorks; however, the approach when solid modeling with any of the aforementioned CAD packages (with the exception of TinkerCAD) will be very similar. We begin by creating a detailed 2D sketch of the model in our chosen CAD package as seen in the following figure:

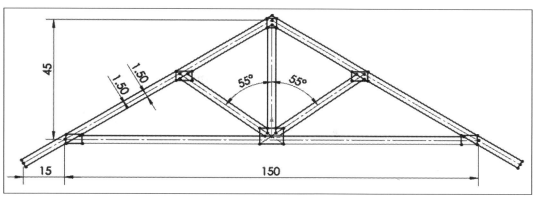

A common roof truss detailed sketch

From this point, we choose what sections of the sketch to extrude and to what distance. Let's give the gussets a 0.4 mm thickness and the beams 1 mm thickness as shown in the following figure:

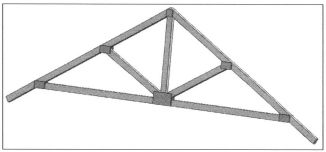

A 3D model for roof truss

There we have it, one roof truss. We began by extruding the back gussets 0.4 mm, then extruded the beams 1 mm, and ended by extruding the front gussets 0.4 mm. From here, all that's left to do is to save our work. We have two possible choices of file format that work well with 3D printing software options, the most common being `.stl` (`.obj` is the second). We'll choose to save this file in the `.stl` format with the name `ch2_roof_truss.stl`.

Summary

In this chapter, we were introduced to several different CAD packages ranging in price and features. We then discussed some basic solid modeling concepts and best practices complete with several design guidelines. This chapter ended with the example of designing a roof truss ready for printing on our MakerBot.

3

3D Printing Software

We will look to answer the question of how a CAD file gets turned into a 3D printed part. In the process we will touch on the different 3D printing software options and discuss many of the 3D printing options useful in printing a part. We will cover the following topics:

- Introducing and discussing the two most common 3D printing software packages: MakerWare and ReplicatorG
- Converting an `.stl` or `.obj` file to `.x3g` or `.s3g`
- Behind the scenes view of how the software breaks down the model into a series of motor movements
- Discussion of influencing print options
- An example on printing the roof truss from *Chapter 2, 3D Modeling Software*

Software choices

If you remember from *Chapter 2, 3D Modeling Software*, we had an abundant number of different modeling software packages from which to choose. Fortunately, in this chapter we are faced with a decision between only two different software packages for converting a model into 3D printer- ready form. These packages are as follows:

- **MakerWare**: This is a software created by MakerBot for use with MakerBot printers
- **ReplicatorG**: This is an open source software for use with any basic FFF printers

But what exactly does this software do, and how does it convert a 3D model from the virtual to the physical world?

3D printing software is improving in leaps and bounds. Do your best to stay up to date with any updates, because these will have enormous effects on your print quality.

Function

The software starts by taking a .stl or .obj file along, with all our settings, and converts it into GCode. Think of the GCode like an instruction set to our printer, which includes where to move, how fast to move, whether or not to extrude material, extruder temperature, lower platform, and so on. The following screenshot shows an example of GCode produced by the ReplicatorG slicing engine Skeinforge at the start of a print:

```
M103 (disable RPM)
M73 P0 (enable build progress)
G21 (set units to mm)
G90 (set positioning to absolute)
M109 S110 T0 (set HBP temperature)
M104 S220 T0 (set extruder temperature) (temp updated by printOMatic)
(**** begin homing ****)
G162 X Y F2500 (home XY axes maximum)
G161 Z F1100 (home Z axis minimum)
G92 Z-5 (set Z to -5)
G1 Z0.0 (move Z to "0")
G161 Z F100 (home Z axis minimum)
M132 X Y Z A B (Recall stored home offsets for XYZAB axis)
(**** end homing ****)
G1 X-110.5 Y-74 Z150 F3300.0 (move to waiting position)
G130 X20 Y20 Z20 A20 B20 (Lower stepper Vrefs while heating)
M6 T0 (wait for toolhead, and HBP to reach temperature)
G130 X127 Y127 Z40 A127 B127 (Set Stepper motor Vref to defaults)
M108 R3.0 T0
G0 X-110.5 Y-74 (Position Nozzle)
G0 Z0.6      (Position Height)
M108 R5.0    (Set Extruder Speed)
M101         (Start Extruder)
G4 P2000     (Create Anchor)
```

Start of GCode

The slicing engine is what tells your printer what to make and exactly how to make it. The algorithm involved directly relates to print quality, and thus gets the most attention from developers. It's at this stage we can see the tradeoff between software and hardware: maybe the printer has the capability to print with greater resolution but current software might only break the model down so far? Or perhaps it's the opposite, where the software can break down the model finer than the hardware is capable of producing? It turns out this is a major factor in what separates personal and commercial printers, and even a $200 and $2,000 printer — precision.

More precision costs more money in both hardware and software development. The hardware must be able to handle the precision calculated in software, and where it cannot, and then software solutions must be implemented in circumvention. It's these reasons why algorithms improve by leaps and bounds with every software update, and why newer released printers outperform their predecessors.

To make it easier on the microcontroller, in the printer the GCode is converted into the `.s3g` or `.x3g` code, which is essentially just optimized GCode. From here it is used to generate motor steps and direction pulses, which are sent to the motor controller and then to the motors. It's at this stage we realize that the process of 3D printing is just a handful of motors moving in a set pattern combined with a heater to melt the plastic material. The magic of 3D printing happens behind the scenes inside the slicing algorithm in order to create those explicit patterns.

MakerWare

You may be thinking, "This software is made by MakerBot and is intended to use with MakerBot printers that sounds like the best option"; well, you are mostly correct. MakerWare is currently still in beta, but is released for general use. The software is always in revision, and has made major improvements in a very short period time.

Logically, it would make sense to use the software explicitly designed for use with your printer, but up until MakerWare v2.2, the ReplicatorG software had been superior. With all the improvements made in MakerWare's latest release v2.3.1, I would argue that the MakerWare software surpasses the ReplicatorG for use with a MakerBot 3D printer. This is one of the joys of being involved with MakerBot and the 3D printing environment- The products are always evolving and always improving. In a period of five years, MakerBot went from an idea to being acquired by Stratasys for $403 million. This speaks for how fast the industry is moving, and how fast the technology is advancing.

For those interested, visit `http://www.makerbot.com/blog/category/makerbot-software-updates/` to see a detailed description (lots of pictures) of the improvements in each MakerWare update.

ReplicatorG

You might be wondering why we would even consider the ReplicatorG software. The simple answer is with the release of MakerWare v2.3.1 and the purchase of a MakerBot, we wouldn't. The ReplicatorG software undoubtedly served as a building block for many of the features in MakerWare, and was the leading software for personal/hobbyist 3D printing for many years. The MakerWare software will meet all the needs for our designs, but if you are interested in learning more about open source 3D printing, I would suggest checking out this software.

We have chosen to use MakerWare (v2.3.1) for the examples in the book, as this software is most tailored to our needs. Visit `http://www.makerbot.com/makerware/` to download your own beta copy.

MakerWare options and settings

The first step after opening MakerWare is to add a model to the build platform by clicking on the Add button. Let's add Mr Jaws (by navigating to **File | Examples | Mr_Jaws.stl**) to our build platform. Once the model has been added, it needs to be selected by left-clicking it. This should highlight the model in yellow as shown in the following screenshot:

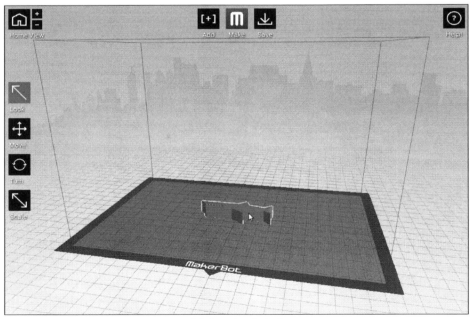

Mr Jaws is selected

Notice the buttons on the left-hand side, which are intuitively labeled **Look, Move, Turn**, and **Scale**. Clicking these buttons allows us to orient our model. Let's move Mr Jaws to the top-right corner, spin him 180 degrees in the Z-plane, and scale him to 110 percent. The result can be seen in the following screenshot:

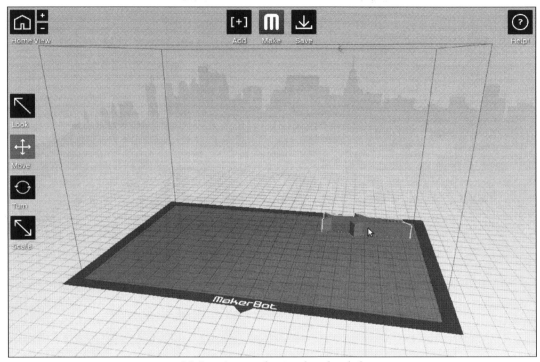

Mr Jaws is moved, rotated, and scaled

Once we are satisfied with the orientation, click on **Make** located at the top of the screen to open up the print options.

Ensure that your model is sitting on the platform by hitting the **On Platform** button (by navigating to **Move | On Platform**); else, you will print many layers of supporting material before finally reaching your part (if your part is floating above the platform), or you will damage your nozzle and platform (if your part is floating below the platform).

Print options

The default options are fairly straightforward, and will modify all the advanced options automatically. We will use the following table to describe each of the default options:

Option	Description
I want to:	This gives the option where to save the file or to send it directly to your MakerBot, if its plugged in by USB.
Export For:	This helps you select your MakerBot.
Material:	This helps you select the PLA that is recommended.
Resolution:	MakerWare has three quick set profiles which are **Low**, **Standard**, and **High**. These profiles reference the desired print resolution and directly control the Z-layer height. Remember that higher resolution requires longer print times.
Raft:	A raft is a surface slightly larger than the part which is built between the bottom of the part and the build platform. Rafts help reduce warping by having more surface area adhered to the build platform. Once a part has been printed, the raft is easily broken away. We will always be using rafts to help reduce errors in our models brought about by poor adhesion and warping.
Supports:	Supports are used to support sharp overhangs. We will always have the support box checked, because the software will determine when and where to use supports and will not print them if they are not needed. This ensures we will never run into errors from floating layers.

By evaluating the advanced options, we are able to observe the result from changing the default options and gain a little more insight into settings that influence our print. The following is a table describing these advanced options:

Advanced options	Description
Profile:	Profiles handle all the settings of a print. Profiles are a grouping of preselected options. By default, there are three profiles: **Low**, **Standard**, and **High,** but you can create your own custom profiles.
Slicer:	The options are between MakerBot Slicer and Skeinforge slicer, and can be changed by creating a new profile. It is recommended that we use the MakerBot slicing engine, because it has been optimized for use with MakerBot printers, as mentioned earlier.

Advanced options	Description
Quality | Infill:	Infill is the density of the object measured by a percentage. By default, the amount of infill is low (less than 20 percent) to save both time and material. The slicing engine will automatically create a pattern for the infill (most commonly honeycomb).
Quality | Number of Shells:	The number of shells will represent the perimeter thickness of your model. One shell corresponds to one layer (which is approximately 0.4 mm the width of the nozzle opening in XY, and will depend on the next property, **Quality | Layer Height**, for the Z thickness). All the profiles default to two shells. If strength is a concern for your model, it is suggested to increase the number of shells rather than infill. Adding shells will also increase print times.
Quality | Layer Height:	Layer height is the height of each individual cross-sectional layer. MakerBot Replicator 2 is capable of heights as low as 0.1 mm. This corresponds to 10 layers for a model of 1 mm in height. Lowering the height will increase print times.
Temperature | Extruders:	The temperature for the extruder by default sets to 230 C. Greater temperatures can improve adhesion but may require slower printing. Every individual has their own "magic number" for temperature, which they feel works best but its best to say within +/- 10 C range of the default. For our models we will be using the default 230 C.
Temperature | Build Plate	A heated build plate is only required if we are printing in ABS, in order to reduce warping. The default is 110 C, and slightly higher temperatures will improve adhesion, but also risk greater warping upon cooling.
Speed | Speed while Extruding:	Extruder speed and temperature are directly linked to one another; the speed needs to be slow enough to allow the layer currently being extruded to bond with the layer underneath. Greater speeds have the potential to reduce accuracy but will decrease print time. Be extremely cautious while modifying this parameter, because it takes experience to match increased speed and temperatures properly.
Speed | Speed while Travelling:	When not extruding, the extruder head is capable of faster travel. It is recommended to leave this parameter as set.
Preview before printing	This is an amazing tool, and you should check it off every time. Preview before printing allows you to see an approximate material use and time estimate to print the given model.

To end our examination of options, we are going to very briefly examine creating a new profile. In creating a new profile, we have direct access to all of the underlying settings. If you are interested, I suggest you visit `www.makerbot.com/support/makerware/documentation/slicer` for a full list of settings we are able to modify. The settings are extremely explicit and give us absolute control over the slicing engine. As an example, one option is `raftBaseDensity` which is set by default to 0.3 (30 percent). Changing this option will adjust the infill used in the creation of our rafts.

 MakerWare lets you create a new profile using a preexisting profile as a base. This is a good approach when we want all the properties of one profile but want to make a few minor changes of our own, rather than creating an entirely new profile from scratch.

Now, let's apply what we have just learned about the settings in MakerWare to print our roof truss (`ch2_roof_truss.stl`) from *Chapter 2, 3D Modeling Software*.

 An excellent video can be found at: `http://www.makerbot.com/support/makerware/videos/`, which recaps traversing the MakerWare settings.

An example – roof truss

We will be using the roof truss we modeled in *Chapter 2, 3D Modeling Software*, and going through the necessary steps in preparation for our first print.

To begin with, let's open MakerWare and add `ch2_roof_truss.stl` to our build platform.

 Sometimes, based on how we have designed the model when we add a file to the build platform, we will be prompted with the pop up shown in the following screenshot. It's best to select **Keep Position** and ensure that we manually orient the part on the build platform at a later time once properly oriented.

How should we orient this part? If we remember in *Chapter 2, 3D Modeling Software*, we designed this model to be printed lying flat against the build platform. Therefore, we will move and turn the object to be oriented as shown in the following screenshot, as this is the orientation anticipated during design:

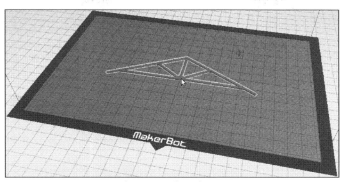

The oriented roof truss

This tip has already been mentioned, but it is so important that it's worth rementioning. Ensure that your model is sitting on the platform by hitting **On Platform** (navigate to **Move | On Platform**); else, you will print many layers of supporting material before finally reaching your part (if your part is floating above the platform), or you will damage your nozzle and platform (if your part is floating below the platform).

Now that we have oriented our part, we are ready to print. Let's click the **Make** button and move on to talking about settings for this print.

1. Select your 3D printer make and material (PLA suggested).
2. Select the checkboxes for **Raft:** and **Supports:**, because we enable these for every print to help reduce errors.
3. Set **Layer Height:** to **0.20 mm**. If we remember, we made our gussets 0.4 mm thick. Therefore, the layer height that would work the best would be 0.1mm, which corresponds to the **High** print resolution (four layers in total). We could also use the default (two layers); however, if we were to use the **High** print resolution, our gussets would then be 0.3mm (one layer) thick instead of the intended 0.4mm, because the MakerBot slicing engine will under apply material rather than over apply. For this example, we should be able to use the **Standard** resolution to save some time. Save the file to the SD card that came with our MakerBot, but we can also connect to our MakerBot directly through USB to print directly by selecting the **Make It Now** option. Saving to SD also reduces the chances that any OS or model complexity issues will corrupt our print.

4. Insert the SD card into the MakerBot, select **Build from SD** from the menu, and choose our file named ch3_roof_truss.s3g. The following screenshot shows our settings:

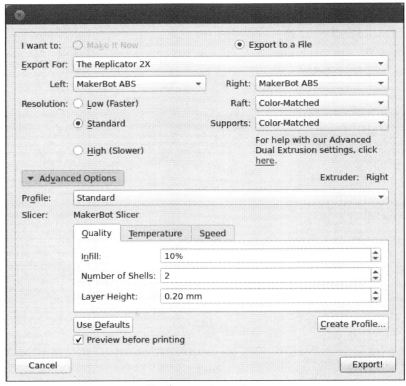

Roof truss print settings

In about 30 minutes our roof truss will be printed. Remove the part from the platform and then break away the raft and any supports. Congratulations, we have printed our first part!

 A fine pair of pliers or a pair of tweezers helps remove the supporting structure.

What you might notice when the part is printing is that it's starting to banana boat a little bit. This is because of the parts geometry; parts that are long and flat along the build platform tend to warp more.

Avoiding warping

There are three main solutions to help reduce warping. First, we can turn the heated build platform to about 40 C (for printing with PLA), which will help the bottom layer of the raft adhere to the platform. The second option is to re-level our build platform. If our nozzle is a little too far away from the platform, the material will cool from its melted state before coming in contact with the layer below it, resulting in poor adhesion. The last solution is an ABS and acetone slurry, which we lay in a very thin layer atop the Kapton tape on our build platform.

Acetone is a good solvent for many plastics, and a 50-50 mixture will break down the ABS to a consistency slightly thinner than molasses. Find a small glass jar (somewhere between 100-200 ml) and fill it approximately three-fourth full with ABS.

 Acetone is poisonous and flammable; use caution while handling, and keep out of reach from children.

Fill the remainder of the glass with acetone and seal the lid. Wait approximately 30 minutes for the acetone to start breaking down the ABS. You should see the plastic inside the jar starting to form into one large blob. Continue adding little bits of acetone until you have reached the desired consistency.

 A great source for slurry plastic is any supporting material from other prints or previous missprints.

To apply the mixture, use an empty pen body, thick plastic straw, or 3D printed solid tube. What's most important while applying the slurry to the Kapton tape is roughly covering the entire area of the print and not having too thick of a layer. Spaces or voids between the slurry are fine. We don't want to apply too thick of a layer, else we risk changing the print height. The following image shows the maximal amount of slurry you would lay; anymore is too much, and you can thin it by carefully applying some acetone:

Slurry maximal thickness

You'll notice after about 10 minutes of sitting on the build platform that the slurry will harden as the acetone evaporates. Left behind are thin deposits of ABS stuck to the Kapton tape, to which our raft will have no problems sticking.

This slurry works well adhering parts to the build platform, but does require extra time to set up. Luckily, you will not use much of the slurry; therefore, one batch should last several months, and you only need to reapply to selected sections where removing the raft also removes the base of slurry (or if you replace the Kapton tape). The mixture is very sticky and contains acetone, so exercise caution while handling.

Ensure to close the lid tightly on your slurry, because exposure to air will cause the acetone to evaporate. If your slurry is too thick, just mix in more acetone.

Removing the part from the platform

You may notice after applying this mixture that the part adheres to the platform so well that you have difficulties during removal. What works well for removing a part that is stuck to the platform is to wedge a butter knife between the raft and the Kapton tape. The butter knife should be dull enough that it does not scrape through the tape and damage your platform, and should also give you a mechanical advantage to remove the part.

Summary

We broke down the process of 3D printing into simple motor responses that coordinate to the intricate cross-sectional pattern created by the slicing engine. The MakerWare software package has improved to a level superior than it's open source counterpart, ReplicatorG, and has been optimized for printing using MakerBot. Therefore, we decided on the MakerWare (v2.3.1) software package for our printing needs. We went on to discuss some of the default and advanced options in detail before getting our hands wet, learning how to add and orient a model on our build plate. This chapter ended by printing our roof truss from the previous chapter and covering two different methods to avoid warping.

In the next chapter we will be adding multiple colors to our roof truss in order to highlight multiple components.

4
Multicolor Design

This chapter covers utilizing the multiple heads on the MakerBot Replicator (Dual Extruder) and Replicator 2X to print a single solid model composed of two different colors. In order to accomplish this, we must first briefly touch on the concept of assemblies and multibody parts before leading into a discussion about the MakerWare settings. Through this chapter, we will be redesigning our roof truss model used in *Chapter 2, 3D Modeling Software*, and *Chapter 3, 3D Printing Software*, which we will print using multiple colors. If you don't have a multihead printer, we also cover how to achieve the same multicolored part via Z Pause, and assemblies.

Assemblies and multibody parts

Look at any of the products around you, and chances are you'll notice that the vast majority of them are composed of one or more parts. As an example, this book (print- based not e-book) has text on pages which are bound together, which are also bound to a cover. If we assemble all these individual components (the pages, the binding, and the cover), we have a new model that is an **assembly** of components.

These components interact with one another in an explicit way, which is something we must specify. Referring back to our book example, the cover must go on the outside of the pages and the binding must attach the pages to both one another and the cover. These are properties of the assembly itself and are known as **mates**. Simple mates specify where in space each model is placed in relation to one another. There are more advanced mates which specify interactions during animation or simulation, but these are outside the scope of our use.

Multibody

Multibody parts in the majority of scenarios are a bad design practice and should be avoided. A multibody part is a single model that has two bodies which do not connect. An example can be seen in the following figure:

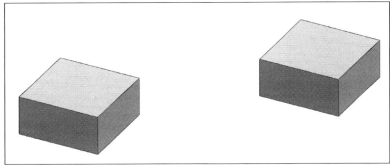

A multibody model

Even though the model has two bodies, it is still considered one part. Certain modeling software allow us to extract each individual body into its own part. This is the software trying to help us adhere to proper design principles.

Experienced designers might use multibody parts to create more complex part geometries, but upon completion the bodies are always exported to individual files.

1 thought per part

This principal is derived from the computer programming principal of "one thought per function".

Color and multimaterial options

In *Chapter 1, A Primer on 3D Printing*, we talked about the two main types of materials and the recommended PLA as our material of choice, because it contracts much less than ABS during cooling. PLA comes in a wide variety of colors, thereby, letting us load separate colors into each of our extruders and print a single solid part in multiple colors. In addition to color, MakerBot also has translucent and glow-in-the-dark PLA. Note that to achieve the desired translucent effects, certain print settings are required (zero infill and a maximum of two shells), which needs to be taken into consideration while designing and printing.

MakerBot is always exploring/incorporating/creating new material options for use with the MakerWare software. The most recent advancement is MakerBot Flexible Filament, which for MakerWare v2.3.1, is only an available material option for The MakerBot Replicator 2.

Redesigning of the roof truss

Let's apply what we have just learned about assemblies and multibody parts to redesign our roof truss model from *Chapter 2, 3D Modeling Software*, and *Chapter 3, 3D Printing Software*, into an assembly.

The level of granularity that we choose will depend on what features we intend to highlight. In this example, we are choosing to highlight the gussets; therefore, we should make these components in their own models. For our wooden components, we could model these all individually and combine them with our gussets, which would be a more accurate representation of the real-world system. However, to reduce time and complexity, in our example we can print the entire wooden structure as one model. Here, we can see a tradeoff between accuracy, detail, time, and complexity, which is decided by which component(s) we are trying to emphasize. If instead of the gussets, we were instead emphasizing the chord or the Web, we might want to model those components individually. More granularity equals more complexity, which in turn equals more time.

Now that we have decided how we are going to model this assembly, let's begin to execute this plan.

1. Extrude the wooden components to 2 mm using the same sketch from *Chapter 2, 3D Modeling Software*. The following image shows both the sketch and extruded product. We'll save the file as ch4_wooden with the extension defaulted by our CAD package. We are using SolidWorks for the examples in this book, so the file will be ch4_wooden.sldprt.

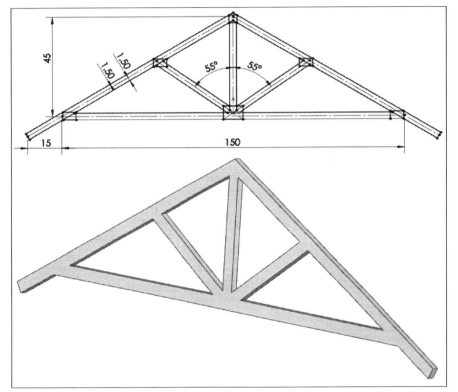

The sketch and wood extrude

2. Next on our agenda is how we want to model the gussets. The first ideas that come to mind are to make a couple of different-sized gussets and perhaps add some top grooves to the gussets to give them a bit of texture. What's important to remember is that increasing complexity increases design and print time. For this example, let's design three different gussets: a large rectangle for connecting the bottom cords and the Web, a square for the very top, and a small rectangle for all the other locations. We'll give the gussets all a depth of 0.5 mm, 0.1mm larger than in *Chapter 2, 3D Modeling Software*. The following image shows dimensions for the three different gussets, which we will label `ch4_gusset_large`, `ch4_gusset_square`, and `ch4_gusset_regular` respectively:

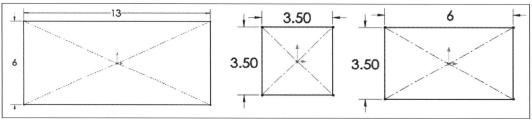

To the left is a large gusset, in the middle is a square gusset, and to the right is a regular gusset

3. Add grooves to our gussets. But how deep should we make them? This will depend under what settings we want to print this part, and also what orientation. If we intend to use the same orientation from *Chapter 2, 3D Modeling Software*, and *Chapter 3, 3D Printing Software*, our Z axis will control our precision, which (if you remember) has a minimum height of 0.1 mm. If our grooves are not at least 0.1 mm deep, there is no guarantee that they will be printed at all even under the highest resolution. Conversely, if they are too deep (greater than 4 mm), there is no guarantee that the bottom will be printed. Any distance in between these maximums (0.1 mm to 0.4 mm) will be printed to the specified resolution.

There is no such way to achieve a precision greater than your specified resolution. Let's use a simple example of a sheet of paper that is 0.13 mm high. If we print this model with a precision of 0.1 mm we it measure afterwards, we will note the height to be 0.1 mm. The same holds true for the XY precision. As we might expect, this is caused by the process of 3D printing – layering material from a 2D cross-sectional outline.

4. Cut the rectangular pattern for our grooves into our large gusset, as shown in the following screenshot. We have limited ourselves to printing this model using a **High** print resolution in order to follow the rule of thumb; that is, a minimum of two print layers. If we wanted to print the piece with a lower resolution, we would need to increase the thickness of our gussets.

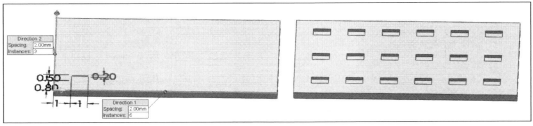

Gusset pattern cuts on a large gusset

5. Create an assembly, insert all the parts, and using mates align the gussets. Our finished product should look equivalent to the roof truss we've used in the previous two chapters; the only difference is that we have an assembly of parts instead of one single part.

6. Not all of the CAD programs have the ability to create assemblies. If your program lacks this ability, don't fret. You still can create multicolor parts either by designing multibodies and then exporting the files individually as we mentioned earlier, or by creating two models in separate files, then being very careful inside MakerWare when we orient the parts.

7. The last step is to save the assembly as individual .stl files, which will create multiple new .stl files—one for each component. Save the assembly as ch4_roof_truss_assembly, and notice the 13 files (all beginning with ch4_roof_truss_assembly_):

   ° ch4_wooden.stl

   ° ch4_roof_truss_gussets_large-1.stl

   ° ch4_roof_truss_gussets_large-2.stl

   ° ch4_roof_truss_gussets_square-1.stl

   ° ch4_roof_truss_gussets_square-2.stl

   ° ch4_roof_truss_gussets_regular-1.stl

   ° ch4_roof_truss_gussets_regular-2.stl

   ° ch4_roof_truss_gussets_regular-3.stl

   ° ch4_roof_truss_gussets_regular-4.stl

- ○ `ch4_roof_truss_gussets_regular-5.stl`
- ○ `ch4_roof_truss_gussets_regular-6.stl`
- ○ `ch4_roof_truss_gussets_regular-7.stl`
- ○ `ch4_roof_truss_gussets_regular-8.stl`

8. We have eight regular gussets in our assembly (four on each side), and each has a different location; therefore, we must create four different `.stl` files. All the files we created should have the parts positioned relative to one another. If not, our only option is to very carefully orient them inside MakerWare. Let's go ahead though; add these files to our MakerWare build platform, and begin exploring how to specify multiple colors.

MakerWare multicolor settings

An excellent guide for using MakerWare to print multicolor parts can be found on the MakerBot website at `http://www.makerbot.com/support/makerware/documentation/dual/`, which will aid in our discussion.

In order to print in multicolors, we need either a MakerBot Replicator (Dual) or Replicator 2X. If you have a single printhead MakerBot machine your only option for multicolor printing is a process called Z Pause, which will be covered near the end of this chapter.

Now we need to select our printer in MakerWare from the Type of MakerBot option (**MakerBots | Type of MakerBot**). Once we select either **The Replicator (Dual)** or **The Replicator 2X**, we notice that an **Object** option appears below the **Scale** option on the left-hand side of the screen. We will get into using this new feature right after we orient our model.

At this point, if you haven't already, you should add all the models to the build platform.

 We touched on this before, but now it's extremely important to select **Keep Position** if prompted with a pop up. Clicking on **Move to Platform** with multiple parts will loose the relationship between parts inside MakerWare. If you do click on this by accident, simply delete the part and re-add it, this time selecting **Keep Position**.

Select all of the models by holding the *Shift* key and left-clicking each model. Once we have all the models selected, we are going to orient the model the same way as we did in *Chapter 3, 3D Printing Software*, by using the **Move** and **Turn** options. We're going to orient the model to the position shown in the following screenshot, which is the print orientation we had optimized for during design:

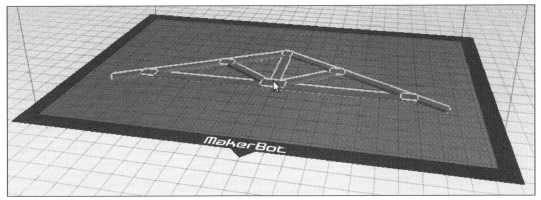

An oriented gusset assembly

If your modeling software doesn't allow for assemblies and you chose to design each part independently (without the use of multi-body parts), it's at this stage you would have to position each component individually inside MakerWare.

Now that we have the model oriented, we are ready to select which extruder should print which objects. Open **Makerware Settings** (by navigating to **Edit | Settings**). Here is where we select the colors that we have loaded in each of our extruders.

We need to tell MakerWare which models go with which extruders by selecting one of our models and left-clicking the **Object** option located to the left-hand side of the screen under **Scale** (this will only appear if we have selected **The Replicator (Dual)** or **The Replicator 2X**. Here we can select the extruder for each of our objects, which will color the objects accordingly. The following screenshot shows our gussets selected as a different extruder as compared to all our gussets:

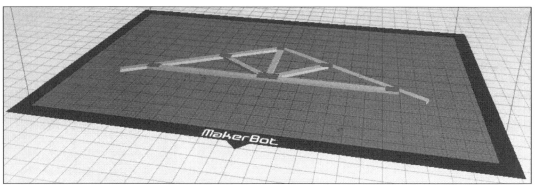

The Dual extruder selection (green and yellow) gusset assembly

Once we are satisfied, we are ready to make. If we do not have a dual-headed MakerBot or if one of our heads is for whatever reason out of commission, we do have one other option for printing in dual colors — Z Pause.

Z Pause

To use Z Pause, we must first make sure we have Firmware 7.3 or above installed on our MakerBot. Z Pause allows us to choose a location (in mm) to pause the print during which we can manually change the filament color in the extruder.

This setting is enabled from the MakerBot interface board itself rather than in MakerWare. During a print, first ensure that you are at the home screen by hitting *Left* on the MakerBot D-Pad, and then scroll down and select **Z Pause**. Choose the height in mm for the filament you want to change. Once the print reaches this height, the printer will pause allowing you to change the filament. After you have changed the filament, hit *Resume*.

Roof truss print settings

We are going to cover some of the options we have if we want to print this model.

Specified supports

MakerWare v2.2 had one major drawback when it came to multicolor printing; we were not able to use rafts or supports. This severely constricted the flexibility in design, as we were not able to print any models with sharp overhangs. The release of MakerWare v2.3.1 fixed this huge issue by introducing rafts and supports, and also allows us to specify which printer head we would like to use for these supporting structures.

If we have a MakerBot Replicator Dual or Replicator 2X, this is the simplest option to achieve multicolor prints.

Z Print

Depending on geometry, we can really benefit from Z Pause. Z Pause has the benefit of rafts and supports while still being able to use multicolors (restricted to changing colors in layers). This allows us (regardless of the number of print heads) to print a model in multiple colors.

Our roof truss would print very well using Z Print. The first 0.5 mm is our first set of gussets, then the next 1.5 mm is our wooden components, and the last 0.5 mm is our second set of gussets. To do this, we need to go back and select only one extruder head for all our parts. Then, use the Z Print setting on the MakerBot, as mentioned in the Z Print section in this chapter — once at 0.5 mm and the second at 2.0 mm (0.5 mm gussets along with 1.5 mm wood).

The last layer of supporting material is sometime difficult to remove from our part, and using multicolors we may unfortunately have some different-colored supporting material attached. If it doesn't affect the look of our part too drastically, what we can do to avoid this is reduce the Z Print height by our **Layer Height**; this way, the last layer of supporting material will be in the color of our new layer. A second option is sandpaper.

Lateral/symmetry splitting

Another option we have is to create a new assembly, as seen in the following image, which is exactly one half of the model. To do this, we need to reduce the extrusion of our wooden component to half and remove all the gussets from one side of the assembly. Both halves are identical, so we only need to print one half twice and then superglue the model back together. The advantage of this technique is that we can use multicolored printing and have our model sit flat on the build platform (we will also have to heat the build platform to ensure adhesion).

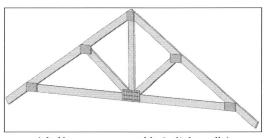

A half root truss assembly (split laterally)

Assembling

The final option is to print all the components separately and again, using superglue, glue all the components into position.

We can add all of our parts to the build platform and print them all in one print, rather than having to print each individually. The following screenshot shows the build platform with all of our parts laid out. This is a very common approach and is known as a **build tray**. All the .stl files are inside the folder ch4_build_tray/.

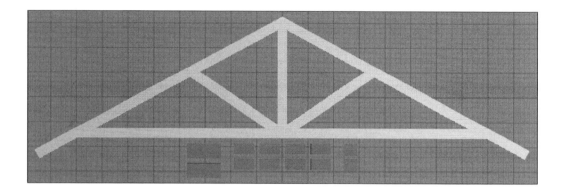

Redesigning

Sometimes, we are faced with no other decision but to slightly redesign the part to facilitate printing. For our example, what we could do is cut a very thin (0.2 mm) square into our wooden model which the gussets will then sit inside. By doing this, we no longer require rafts or supports in our model, because the wooden component will sit flush against the build platform.

Print settings

Regardless of the option chosen, our last step before printing is determining which resolution to use. Looking at our model, the only area of concern is the gusset grooves. If you remember, we made these 0.2 mm deep leaving 0.3 mm of material. We also made the gussets themselves 0.5 mm thick. Our rule of thumb is to have at absolute minimum two layers of thickness; therefore, we have no other choice than to print using high resolution. If we wanted to print on a standing resolution, we should modify our gusset, as we noted earlier, because they are the components that are dictating our resolution.

What's important to note once our print is done is the pattern on the large gusset. If you look very closely, you'll see that indeed the top of the gusset has the pattern we had outlined; however, it looks nowhere near as was on our screen during modeling. *What you design isn't always what you'll get*. This is a good example of us pushing the absolute limits of our MakerBot's resolution expecting something that on screen has actually been highly magnified. The fault falls on us the designer, not on the printer.

Congratulations, we have just created and assembled our first multicolor part! We are now ready to move on to more complicated assemblies, which we will cover in the next chapter.

Summary

This chapter began by introducing us to assemblies and multibody parts. We then applied these concepts in order to redesign our roof truss model that we've used through the previous two chapters into an assembly. Next, we added the roof truss to MakerWare and went through the necessary steps selecting the colors for each component and specifying build settings. We ended by showing multiple ways by which we could print multicolored parts that depend on our MakerBot. In the next chapter we will be going into more detailed assemblies and will introduce the concept of tolerancing in order to create larger, more complex assemblies.

5
Multipart Design

This chapter will prepare us for creating more advanced assemblies by introducing the concepts of tolerancing and designing for assembly. In this chapter, we will cover the following topics:

- Creating more advanced assemblies
- Incorporating more challenging part geometry and a greater number of components
- Learning how component fits and tolerancing aid in the physical assembly of our parts
- Understanding what it means to design for assembly
- An example on designing an office building facade with interchangeable components

Introducing tolerancing and fits

Without significantly affecting function, certain dimensions, properties, or conditions may vary within a set limit; this is known as **tolerance**. Tolerance gives leeway for imperfections without compromising performance. Our MakerBot has a tolerance of +/- 11 microns in XY and +/- 5 microns in Z. An example for this could be to design a cube with the specifications 1 mm for X x 1 mm for Y x 1 mm for Z. After printing, the cube will actually be anywhere from 0.989-1.011 mm for X x 0.989-1.011 mm for Y x 0.995-1.005 mm for Z. This tolerance should more than suffice for any of our applications, but what's important to keep in mind is that what we design is not exactly what we get; no machine is capable of perfection. Additionally, even if we had a perfect machine variation in the filament composition, diameter and other environmental factors (such as air moisture) will also affect tolerance.

Fits are intended clearance or interference between components. The type of fit is the responsibility of the designer and will vary between applications. To explain the different types of fits, we are going to use the example of a shaft in a hole, because these are the most common and the simplest two components to fit. All fits can be grouped into three broad categories: **clearance fits**, **interference fits**, and **transition fits**.

The clearance fit

Also known as the **sliding fit**, this type of fit allows full movement of the shaft inside the hole. This type of fit is characterized by a large differential between the shaft and the hole, which can be achieved by either oversizing the hole, under sizing the shaft, or both. The following figure shows an example of a clearance fit:

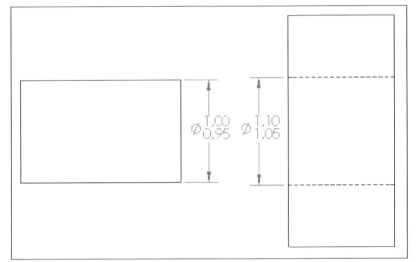

The clearance fit

The interference fit

Also known as the **force fit** or the **press fit**, this type of fit securely holds the shaft in the hole allowing no movement. This type of fit is characterized by a negative differential between the shaft and the hole; the shaft will be larger than the hole and require either some means of force or a heating and cooling/shrinking method to fit into the hole. It is the frictional forces between the shaft and hole that is intended to hold the pieces together. Interference fits are not intended to be disassembled, and having to do so most commonly results in damage to one or both of the components. The following figure shows an example of an interference fit:

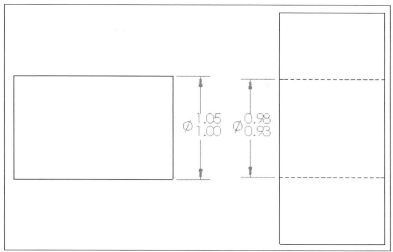

The interference fit

The transition fit

This type of fit is a compromise between clearance and interference. The shaft will be held securely within the hole and will also have the ability to be removed without damage. For our use with the MakerBot, a transition fit will be when we do not use any tolerancing. The following figure illustrates an example of a transition fit:

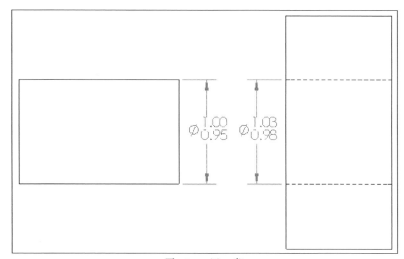

The transition fit

Holes in MakerBot

Before we can go on to talk about which fits work best with our MakerBot, we must first stop and learn how the slicing engine prepares holes. To do this, we are going to print a very simple rectangular block with a hole in its center, but stop this print at about half way. The following image shows the resulting part that was printed using the **Standard** resolution and two shells:

Two shells and infill

Notice that around our hole, two layers of materials were laid which corresponds to the two shells parameter under **Quality** in **Make | Advanced Options**. After those two layers, our infill pattern fills the remainder of the space between the edges of the hole and perimeter of the model. Therefore, in terms of strength, for our hole we have the two bottom layers (and top if it's a through hole) which are entirely filled (the height of those layers will be determined by our resolution), then for the remainder of the hole, we have only a depth of 0.8 mm (0.4 mm multiplied by two layers) followed by infill. Remember that we also have control over the infill percentage under **Make | Advanced Options | Infill**.

If we are to try and force an interference fit, we will most likely damage, at minimum, one layer of the hole. If one layer of the hole is compromised (essentially 50 percent of the holes thickness), the remaining layers' strength will be significantly reduced and may or may not retain the circular shape. By adding more shells, we increase the strength of the hole and reduce the likelihood of extensive deformation. This will also add to print time dependent on part geometry — more complicated part geometry will have significant time addition.

For 99 percent of applications, clearance or transition fits will suffice. The tightest fit we will ever use is a transition with zero clearance (the same dimension for both the shaft and hole). We can use superglue to fuse plastic components together instead of having to use an interference fit. If we find our clearances are too fine, we can use some sandpaper to shave away a bit of material.

The clearance guide

The files `ch5_clearance_guide_holes.stl` and `ch5_clearance_guide_shaft.stl` are extremely useful, because they show several different clearances for one size of shaft. This print serves as a very useful tool when we're deciding on clearances. The shaft has a diameter of 20 mm, and the hole diameters are listed on the guide decreasing in size by 0.05 mm. The following image shows the hole clearance guide:

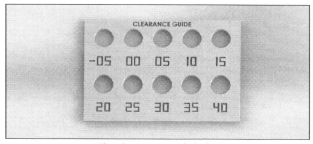

The clearance guide holes

 We will need to reprint the guides so often, as over time both will deform through use.

Designing for assembly

Now that we understand how to fit components together, we are well on our way to creating more intricate assemblies. When we are creating parts that will fit together, we need to consider the process for assembling these parts, else we can run into the problem of designing something that in the real world, can never be assembled. As an example, let's look at the box in the following image:

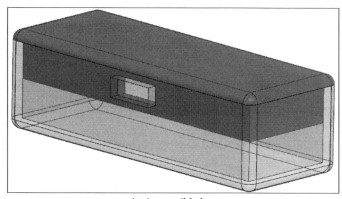

An impossible box

The holes at the front of the box are intended through which to run wires. We can see that once the box has been assembled, the holes on the top piece and bottom piece line up. However, when we think about this, practically there is no physical way for us to remove the top once the wires are routed through the holes. This counteracts our intended function. A quick redesign can be seen in the following image, where we shorten the top and thus eliminate the impossible assembly:

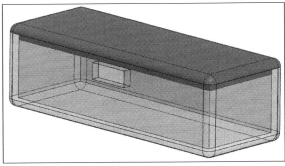

A possible box

Designing for assembly also looks to minimize the total number of components. The simplest solution is the best solution; unnecessary complexity should be avoided. More components cost us more design time, assembly time, part costs, and introduces an unnecessary headache in our project. Spend the extra five minutes really thinking through the design, and once you have your assembly completed, take a step back and try to see if there's a way to reduce the part count.

An example – building facade assembly

Arguably, the most important part of any project is right at the beginning when we are deciding the project scope. If the scope is too large, the project risks going over time, budget, or both. If the scope is too small, the project loses depth and may not cover the intended content extensively enough.

Establishing the project scope

For our example, we are going to create the facade for a subsection of an office building, one of the intermediate stories, and one unit. We want to present several different facades; therefore, we are going to create an assembly where we can combine individual components rather than designing *n* number of different static options. This way, we enable one piece to be used across multiple designs, increasing the number of possible design configurations while reducing the total number of parts. With this method, we are also able to integrate new components much easier across all designs.

As the designer, we now decide how much detail to include, in this case, by specifying the number of components that will create our assembly. We'll decide on three different parts:

- Windows
- Veneer
- Details

Now the question arises, how are we combining these components to create a facade and how many possible facades are we looking to showcase? In order to answer these questions, we need to go into a little more detail for each of our different parts.

Part 1 – windows

From building to building, the window shape can vary immensely. What is common is that a window sits behind a frame or some other type of supporting structure. We can choose to set our window pane as the background onto which for the other structures to assemble. The other components will sit in front of the window and set its shape. Therefore, we only have one possible part for the window, which will also be our background component. Let's make the background cover one unit and be square in shape.

We are able to make this generalization because we are interested in showing the facade of the building, rather than the accurate component makeup. If this model's intended use was for a parts list or BIM validation, we would have to redesign this component.

Part 2 – veneer

These components will sit on top of the window, shape the window, and provide their own structure. There are so many different options for this component, but let's narrow the scope down to three options in window size and two options for our veneer. Our choices are listed here:

- A maximal-sized square window

  This could be designed using a flat (concrete/stucco) structure

- A minimal-sized rectangular window

  This could be designed using bricks or flat (concrete/stucco)

- An intermediate-sized rectangular window

  This could be designed using bricks or flat (concrete/stucco)

Note that we immediately eliminated one option for our maximal-sized square windows because brick seemed inappropriate for this style.

Now, we need to create a way for this component to attach to the window. We're going to use a shaft and hole connection because this is the most simple and will work well in this application. But should the hole be on the background or our component? Technically, it could go on either, but putting the hole on the background will save us some headaches. Why? On the background we can just use a through hole, whereas on the component we need to specify a depth allowing for at least two layers of material thickness. Additionally, with the hole on the component, depending on the part's geometry and orientation, we might have to remove some supporting material that's filled inside the hole.

We should also decide how much clearance we need. From reviewing our clearance guide model, we have decided on 0.1 mm of clearance, which will provide a snug fit and also allow removal without damage.

Part 3 – details

Potential details for the facade of a building are seemly infinite. Let's give only one option, which will be to add a very simple window frame. Again, we have to now decide how to attach this component. We'll use a zero clearance condition (transition fit) and press the window component in place.

Outlining the design layout

Our scope is well defined, and we have broken down our components into the following parts:

- Layer 1 – the background/window

  This is a large square component with holes for shaft inserts

- Layer 2 – the window size and shape

  This could be a maximal-sized square window, an intermediate-sized rectangular window, or a minimal-sized rectangular window

- Layer 3 – veneer

  This could be designed using bricks or flat (concrete/stucco)

- Layer 4 – details

  This indicates the window frame

We can quickly see how, even with a small number of options, we have a large number of possible combinations. Therefore, we need to be exact in where we give variability in order to maintain a reasonable project scope and component count.

Beginning with our first layer, let's go through and design each of these components with proper fits and connections.

Layer 1 – the background/window

Our background will help determine size. Let's use a 100 mm x 100 mm square to represent our section. We could attach these background components together if we wanted to show more than one unit. However, if we were to do this, we might consider adjusting our scale. Using this scale, our parts will take roughly between 1-2 hours each to print under a Normal resolution.

Next, we need to consider how components will attach to this piece. As mentioned earlier, we are going to use a through hole and have shafts on the back of the layers that come in front. But where should we place the holes? Looking forward, regardless of the window shape, we will always have material around the perimeter; therefore, this is a good starting point to place some holes. Let's also use square holes, because they go better with the part's geometry. Lastly, we'll size and position them according to the following figure (2 mm away from the edge using a 4 mm square and a depth of 5 mm):

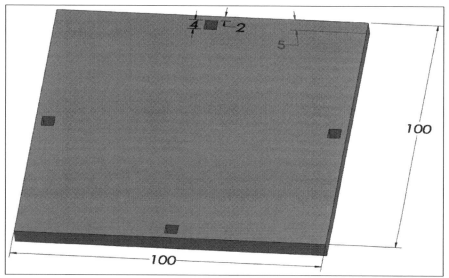

Background/window

Save the part as `ch5_background.stl`. We can use either the **Standard** or **Low** resolution for this print as it doesn't have any complex geometry.

Layer 2 – the window size and shape

This component is responsible for shaping the window and also providing a surface to which both layers 3 and 4 will attach. First and foremost, we should design our window shapes and attachments into our window/background. The following image shows the end results for all three possibilities:

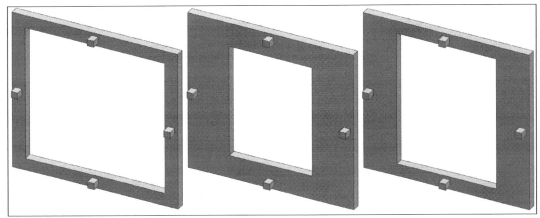

To the left is a maximal-sized square window, in the middle is an intermediate-sized rectangular window, and to the right is a minimal-sized rectangular window

We need some holes to attach the third layer onto this layer, but where should we put those? Also, we'll need to decide how deep the holes should go, as we can't just use a through hole again. Let's take a step back, and think if there is any easier way we can design this.

We need to place holes in layer 2 to support layer 3. Our model requires both layer 2 and layer 3 to properly shape it; therefore, we know that every time we assemble this model, we will have a layer 3 sitting on top of layer 2. Knowing this, instead of having our shafts on layers 2 and 3, we can simply remove the shafts in layer 2 and replace them with a through hole that lines up with layer 1. Then, we'll extend the shafts on layer 3 to go through both layers 2 and 1, lining up all our components. By doing this, we have eliminated some unnecessary complexity and saved print time. Our new layer 2 components and all dimensions are shown in the following image which are extruded 5 mm:

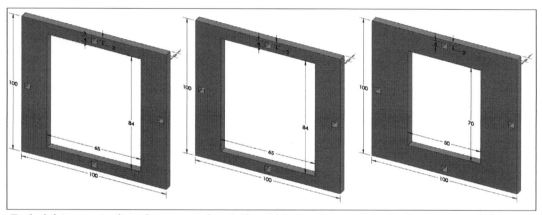

To the left is a maximal-sized square window, in the middle is an intermediate-sized rectangular window, and to the right is a minimal-sized rectangular window

Save these files as ch5_maximal_sized_square_window.stl, ch5_intermediate_sized_square_window, and ch5_minimal_sized_rectangular_window.stl. We are able to use either the **Standard** or **Low** resolution for each of these prints.

Because we made our background and holes perfectly square, we are also able to rotate our windows and have vertically rectangular windows. However, note that if we intend to use this orientation, we should also create additional variations for layers 3 and 4.

Layer 3 – veneer

As mentioned in the last section, this component will have the shaft that will connect through layers 2 and 1. Referencing our guide, we are going to use a clearance of 0.1 mm, because we want this component to remain tight and hold the other components in place. Our two brick models are shown in the following image (remembering that brick was not an option for the maximal-sized square window):

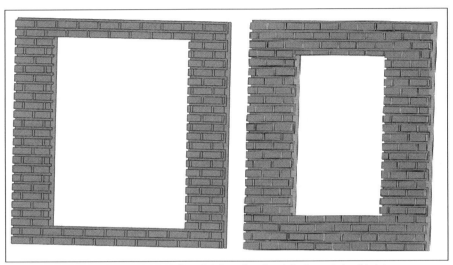

To the left is an intermediate brick and to the right is a minimal brick

Our models using flats are shown in the following image (make sure that the formatting corresponds with the window designed using flats). Note that the leftmost image in the following figure is specially designed for the maximal-sized square window:

To the left is a maximal flat, in the middle is an intermediate flat, and to the right is a minimal flat

Note that none of our veneers have shafts attached. This is because if we were to add the shaft, when we went to print, these parts we would have 10 mm of wasted support material between the shaft and the back face of the veneers. Instead, we will print a 2 mm deep hole, print the shaft separately, insert it into the hole, and then super glue the pieces together.

The files are saved as `ch5_intermediate_brick.stl`, `ch5_minimal_brick.stl`, `ch5_maximal_flat.stl`, `ch5_intermediate_flat.stl`, `ch5_minimal_flat.stl`, and `ch5_veneer_shafts.stl`. Note that each model will require four shafts.

This component is slightly more intricate than layers 1 or 2, but still doesn't have enough complexity to justify the **High** resolution; use the **Standard** or **Low** resolution.

Layer 4 – details

The last component we need to design is our window frame. Our design can be seen in the following figure, which is a very plain border set to fit around the inside the window:

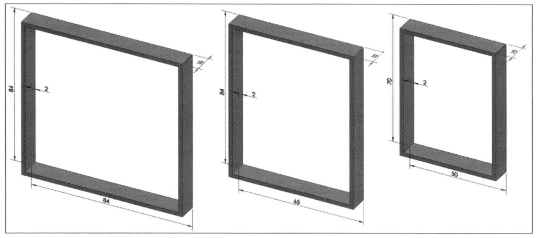

To the left is a maximal frame, in the middle is an intermediate frame, and to the right is a minimal frame

Adding an additional part

We aren't restricted to simple designs; the sky is the limit in terms of design potential. The file `ch5_intricate_desing.stl` is an intricate design for a stone facade attached to our frame. It is intended to be used with the minimal-sized rectangular window, printed using the High resolution, and then super glued onto `ch5_minimal_frame`. The piece is shown in the following figure:

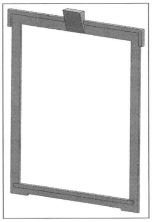

Intricate frame addition

Assembling the layers

Assembly should be easy as all the components should fit snuggly into one another, thanks to our use of clearances. The following image shows assembly for the combination of minimal-sized rectangular window, brick, frame, and the additional part:

Assembly

What's important to take away is that our focus was on what we classified to be an individual unit of the facade. If we were more interested in modeling the entire office building facade, our scale would be much different, and we might choose to combine more assemblies into individual parts in order to reduce our total part count. Our entire assembly for this chapter then could have been printed as one single part either by Z Print or multicolored parts (if we remove the square holes).

Summary

In this chapter, we covered more advanced assemblies, and introduced the concept of component tolerance and fits. We then went on to explore what it means to design for assembly. The majority of this chapter focused on applying these newly learned principles to the practical example of designing a modular unit of an office building facade composed of interchangeable components. Although our example only covered a brief number of possibilities, it can be used as a framework to create infinitely more of them; however, all these things take time to design. We could dramatically reduce design time if we had some sort of library of already designed models that were ready for printing. In the next chapter, we will introduce you to this library, which is found on Thingiverse and GrabCAD. Welcome to the community.

6
The Community – Thingiverse and GrabCAD

This chapter introduces us to the open source community and how to find, edit, and insert parts created by this community into our design. We will also cover the following topics:

- Introducing two extensive free CAD websites (Thingiverse and GrabCAD)
- Finding, analyzing, and licensing restrictions of a model
- An example on finding and modifying a bathroom sink

3D printing web resources

The design/3D printing community is such a powerful resource. With consumer 3D printing being relatively new, the number of free 3D printer-ready files that are available is astonishing. Sites such as Shapeways offer designs and printing at a cost, as does the giant eBay website, who has recently opened its own 3D printing marketplace. But, we are more interested in sites that offer free designs, and two of the leaders in this department are **Thingiverse** and **GrabCAD**, who have collections of hundreds of thousands of models and parts.

Thingiverse

Thingiverse is best explained by the description on their website (`http://www.thingiverse.com/about`):

> *"Thingiverse is a place for you to share your digital designs with the world. We believe that just as computing shifted away from the mainframe into the personal computer that you use today, digital fabrication will share the same path. In fact, it is already happening: laser cutters, cnc machines, 3D printers, and even automated paper cutters are all getting cheaper by the day. These machines are useful for a huge variety of things, but you need to supply them with a digital design in order to get anything useful out of them. We're hoping that together we can create a community of people who create and share designs freely, so that all can benefit from them."*

Thingiverse really is a beautiful idea. It's a website that promotes the sharing of digital designs to everyone and anyone, so that the community as a whole can benefit. We'll have to make an account if we want to actually download any of the models, so we'll do that first before continuing on.

Maneuvering through Thingiverse

Visiting the main page at `www.thingiverse.com`, we should see the website as shown in the following screenshot (although many of the examples may have changed from the time of writing this book):

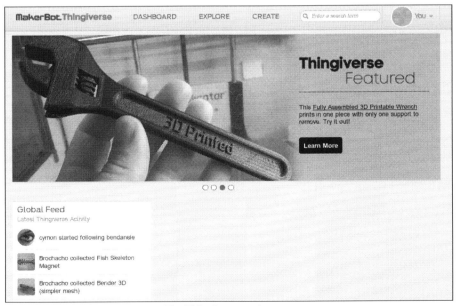

The Thingiverse main page

Feel free to explore the website, but we're interested in searching for the particular topic of toilets. Go to the top-right corner and search `toilet`, which will bring up a page similar to the one seen in the following screenshot:

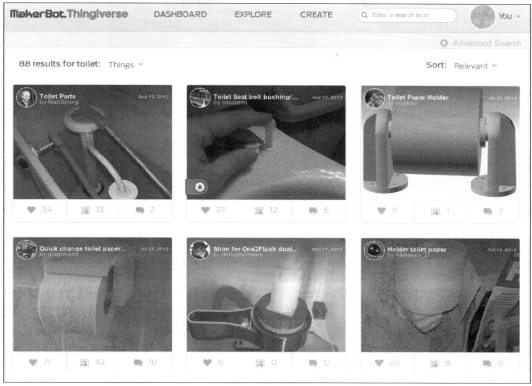

Thingiverse search term—toilet

This will bring up many search results for different toilet parts, toilet paper roll holders, and so on, but what we are interested in is a model of a toilet. Keep looking through the results until you have found the file **Toilet Ornament** by the user **haihuynh**. We will left-click the image, and will now see the following detailed model screen, which provides us with a wealth of information:

Toilet Ornament

On the right-hand side of the image, some of the most important pieces of information are shown, including how many people like this model, how many have made it themselves, and how many have remixed the model. With these three pieces of information, we can quickly get a picture of how successful the model is to print and how other users in the community view the model.

At the bottom of the figure, there are a number of other pictures we can view, which are most commonly the CAD model, the model inside MakerWare (to usually show the different build trays/orientations), and the finished product. When we are ready to download a model, we just click on the big **Download This Thing!** button.

If we scroll down on the page, we are presented with even more information about the model, as seen in the following screenshot. We've labeled some of the most important sections, which we will go over.

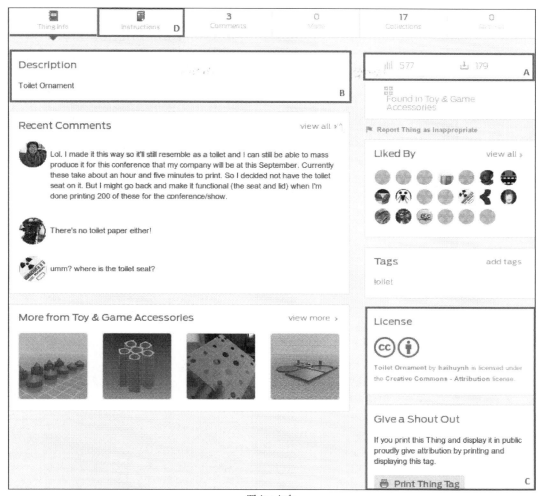

Thing info

The section highlighted as **A** shows us the number of views and downloads this model has received. The higher these numbers are, the more popular a particular model is among the community. This usually translates to models that are of a higher quality.

The section highlighted as **B** is a description by the user. Usually, this section will be filled with any useful information about the model.

The section highlighted as **C** is the license section; we will talk more about this shortly.

Lastly, clicking on **Instructions** in the section highlighted as **D** will take us to an instruction set that generally contains information about printing and assembling the model.

Licensing of Thingiverse models

The specific type of licensing helps us know whether we can copy, distribute, edit, remix, or build upon the given model. We must be very cautious about licensing, because the **Creative Commons** licensing allows the creators of the model to keep copyright of their work but grant others certain permissions. Therefore, if we do not intend to break copyright law, we should read this section carefully for each model we download.

Disclaimer

This does not constitute legal advice; copyright law varies between jurisdictions and doesn't touch on trademarks or patents. Proceed with caution. *It Will Be Awesome If They Don't Screw It Up* by *Michael Weinberg* at `http://publicknowledge.org/it-will-be-awesome-if-they-dont-screw-it-up` is a useful resource.

A very good explanation of the different copyright laws used by Thingiverse in particular can be found at `http://creativecommons.org/licenses/`. We will briefly touch on the most common ones found on Thingiverse.

Attribution

This is perhaps the most common license you will see. Attribution entails the work is free to be used and modified for both personal and commercial use, but you must attribute the work to the author. Attribution is also the most accommodating licensing.

Attribution-ShareAlike

Closely related to Attribution, the Attribution-ShareAlike license adds that if you alter, build on, or transform this work, the resulting model must be shared under the same or a similar license. Essentially, this means that you cannot use a restrictive license on any work you have modified that originally had a ShareAlike license.

Attribution-NonCommercial

The license that we must look out for is the Attribution-NonCommercial licensing. Because our intended use of these parts is for a presentation showpiece, which according to Thingiverse Help Services is considered a promotional material and therefore commercial, we are not able to use models with this type of licensing without explicit permission from the creator.

 An e-mail with personal permission from the creator overrides any sort of licensing on the model. So if there's a model you really want to use, send an e-mail to the creator explaining what your intended use is. People in the community tend to be very accommodating.

GrabCAD

GrabCAD has a very different community as compared to Thingiverse. GrabCAD is focused on CAD models more-so than 3D printing; rarely will we find build instructions or build trays on GrabCAD. What we will find, however, are more complex models and assemblies. Even better yet, each of these models is usually available in several different CAD formats. By having the native format, we are able to actually see a design tree or make modifications right to the original design. This not only helps with remixing but it also helps us learn how these models were created.

Again, before we are actually able to download models, we need to create an account, so we'll do that now before continuing on.

Maneuvering through GrabCAD

After registering, visiting the main page at www.grabcad.com should bring up a web page similar to the one seen in the following screenshot (although, again, many of the examples may have changed since the time this book came into print):

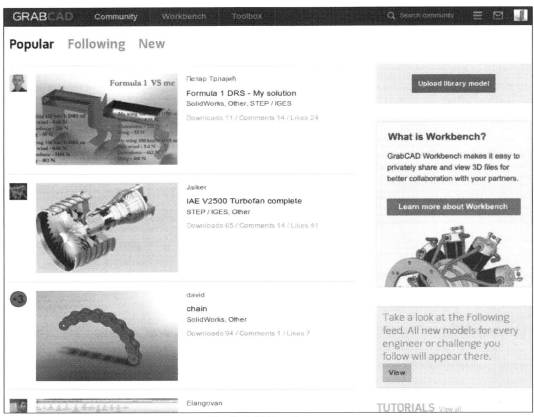

The GrabCAD main page

Similar to Thingiverse, in the top-right corner, we need to type in our search term, which will again be `toilet`. After searching, we will select **Sort by: | Most downloaded**. This is one way to ensure that we see quality models first. We'll select the model **Water Closet** by **Al Trice**, which will take us to the model page as seen in the following screenshot:

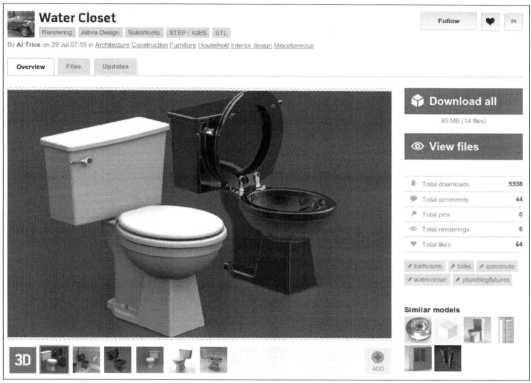

The GrabCAD water closet

GrabCAD also has advanced search options from which you can choose more than 50 different file formats.

This page is strikingly similar to Thingiverse, with important download information to the right and images near the bottom. However, note that the high quality of the images/models is far superior to that of Thingiverse. By clicking on the **Files** tab, we are taken to the page seen in in the following screenshot:

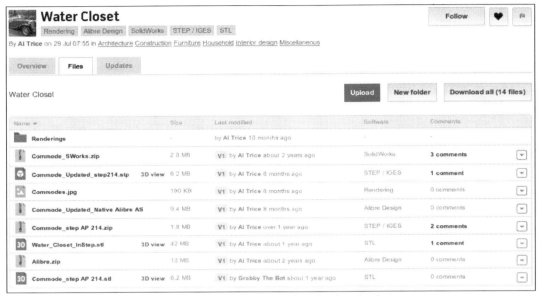

The GrabCAD water closet files for download

Here, we can see all the available files for download. What's important to note is the native file formats that are available (also seen to the top left, immediately beneath the file name beside the user's profile). More popular files will generally accommodate more native file formats, as other users in the community will help translate the files into many formats, giving a wider range of members' access to native formats. One drawback to GradCAD at the current moment, however, is how they do licensing.

Licensing of GrabCAD models

Currently, GrabCAD has no licensing displayed on users' models; however, this in no way means that there are none. Reading through their terms and conditions and speaking with GrabCAD customer support, improved licensing is coming in a very similar manner to Thingiverse. In the meantime, what we'll have to do to get permission to use models commercially (promotional material), is to send the creator an e-mail asking for their permission. The community around GrabCAD is very accommodating, because the site is intended for sharing models; however, just to cover ourselves legally, we simply must ask for permission if we intend to use a model for commercial purposes.

An example – bathroom sink

We'll begin by searching Thingiverse for a bathroom sink/vanity. A quick search yields models for soap dishes, toothbrush holders, and filters—not exactly for what we were searching. Let's try the same search on GrabCAD. This search yields much more promising results. We'll select the model **Bathroom Sink assembly** by **Emil.Rindell**.

Looking at the file types, we see **IronCAD 2011, STEP/IGES, Rendering, STL**, and **Other**. We aren't using IronCAD 2011, therefore, we won't have access to the native file type. However, he has provided `.step`/`.iges` that is a universal file type, along with `.stl`, which is our print-ready format. Let's download the model, and then look at `.stl` in MakerWare as shown in the following screenshot:

Bathroom Sink assembly in MakerWare

 Notice that the description says, "This is the first subassembly to a bathroom design project. Will add some more parts and better renderings later on. Feel free to use this."

Notice how the creator has chosen to model the sink attached to a back surface. We are just interested in the sink, so we'll need to modify this model to be only the sink.

Let's start by opening the .step file in our CAD package. From here, we are able to make changes to the part's geometry. Let's remove everything that isn't the sink/vanity, and we should be left with the model, as shown in the following image:

The sink from Bathroom Sink assembly

Next, we need to prepare this model to be printed. To do this, we need to check that we have a minimum wall thickness of 0.8 mm in XY and 0.2 mm in Z. Also, to make life easier on our printer, we can remove complexities such as the faucet and handles on the drawers in this example (depending on the size we intend to print).

Looking at the model more closely, we notice that the sink is below our minimum wall thickness, as is the back of the storage component. The following image shows these components before and after modification to increase thickness:

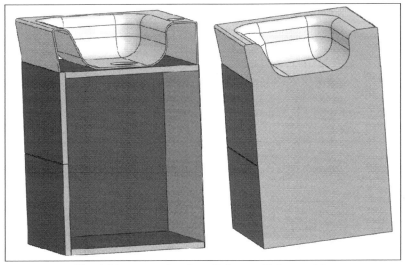

The sink's cross section from Bathroom Sink assembly

The model is nearly ready to print. We should scale the model in our CAD software so that we can measure and ensure our wall thickness remains above the minimum. The scale value should be 0.15.

We've saved the file as `ch7_sink_print_ready.stl`, which we will import into MakerWare and print using the **Standard** print resolution. Note that this model is a prime candidate for Z Print if we want our sink to be of a different color from our cabinet.

Congratulations! We have just edited and printed a model from GrabCAD!

Summary

In this chapter, we learned how to traverse through two extremely valuable free model databases—Thingiverse and GrabCAD. We learned about licensing and worked through a practical example of finding and modifying a model for a vanity.

In the next chapter, we will be applying everything we have learned thus far in our culminating example, working through iterations of a floor plan.

7
Iterative Design

In this final chapter, we will start by introducing iterative design, which is the process of prototyping, testing, analyzing, and refining. Iterative design looks to improve the quality of a design via testing and analysis of a prototype at each iteration. Using this iterative process, we design our culminating example a one-bedroom, one-bathroom apartment floor layout. We will cover the following topics:

- A culminating example on the floor plan
- Rapid iterations of a floor plan by 3D printing simplified models
- Increasing the size and complexity by converting the floor plan into an assembly
- Adding details to the floor plan via staging the bathroom

Usage of iterative design

Traditional iterative design was used with product design teams where, for every major release, a prototype was made, examined, and then refined. This was the application that 3D printing first sought to revolutionize. By utilizing 3D printing, designers were able to reduce the time between revisions, speeding up R&D, and reducing costs associated with prototyping.

The same iterative design is also common in software development, which goes by the name **agile development**. In agile development, developers deliver and review a prototype, either within their team or sometimes also with the customer. The review process allows for feedback, which is used as material for the next iteration. The process repeats until everyone is satisfied.

What's exciting is that the field of architecture has been evolving over the past several years, as more emphasis is being put on the need for 3D modeling. 3D modeling has many benefits, including better visualization for all types of buildings, better error checking, virtual walkthroughs and tours, stunning marketing and promotional tools, and improved coordination between architects, engineers, and contractors. Unfortunately, up until recently, creating a prototype was extremely time-consuming, and required a fair amount of artistic skill, but those who did have the skills and the time to invest would stand out above the competition. This is where 3D printing comes into architecture — to give an architect an unfair advantage over their competition.

2D drawings and 3D CAD models can only go so far; not everyone can take the virtual model or image and relate this to the real world. Also, who's to say that the beautiful building we have designed will actually look as it does on the computer screen, maintain the functionality we've outlined, or most importantly, meet the client's needs. By utilizing 3D printing and an iterative design approach, we allow for maximal client comprehension and more beneficial feedback.

A culminating example – the floor plan

We will be designing the floor plan for a single-story one bedroom, one bathroom apartment.

Initial design

To start with, let's create a drawing for our floor plan, as shown in the following figure with some basic room sizes:

Sketch 1

We have two options for scaling our model: choosing a scale at the beginning and model accordingly, or using the real scale in our CAD package and then scale the model for printing. We'll choose to use the true scale in our CAD model, and then scale accordingly in order to print. While using this method of scaling, we must be careful to ensure we have thick enough walls to print.

We'll make a drawing from our sketch inside our CAD package, and then extrude the walls to 8 ft or 2.43 m, as shown in the following figure. Save this file as `ch7_initial_design.stl`.

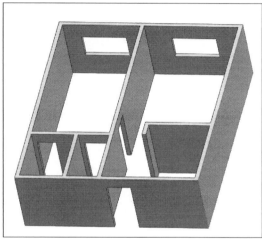

The CAD model from sketch 1

The next challenge we face is printing this model, because in its current state it is obviously too large for our build platform. But we must now decide what scale we want our model to be. For our initial design, let's explore the option of scaling the model to fill half of the build platform in order to minimize print time and eliminate the need for assembly. Set the value of scale to `0.0125` (or 1:80 scale). The purpose of printing the model at this stage is to verify room placement and room size proportionality; therefore, scaling the model to fit half of the build platform is a viable option. A scale of 1:64 would fill the build platform and would take about 1-2 hours longer to print than with our 1:80. We can choose to either scale the model in our CAD package or scale it in MakerWare. As good practice using the MakerWare tools, we will choose to scale the model in MakerWare.

The orientation for the model can be seen in the following screenshot. We'll print this model using the **Standard** resolution. The file is saved as `ch7_origional.stl`.

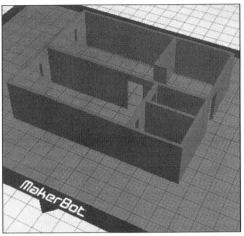

MakerWare model 1

Upon closer inspection, the layout appears awkward having to go through the bedroom to get to the sole bathroom. On paper, this might have seemed fine; however, after examining the crude prototype, we see that we should probably go back and change the floor plan.

A to-scale model person is an extremely useful tool that can be used to help judge sizing. The file `ch7_6ft_person.stl` is a 6 ft tall, 2 ft wide model person that we can scale to fit our needs.

Initial iteration

For our first iteration, let's move the bathroom to a location where it is more accessible, as seen in the following figure:

Iteration 1 — bathroom located in the center

We'll scale and print this model using the same settings as the initial design. The following screenshot shows the first iteration model, which we've saved as ch7_iteration1.stl:

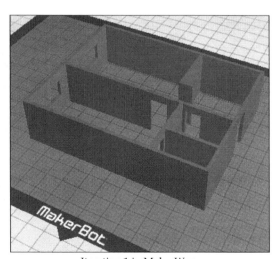

Iteration 1 in MakerWare

There's a much better flow, but our bathroom seems a bit small in comparison to the 10 x 20 bedroom. In our next iteration, let's increase the size of the bathroom.

Second iteration

The following figure shows the updated floor plan sketch incorporating the increase in size by 2 feet of the bathroom and closet. Also (not seen), we've decided to increase the width of the walk-in closet from 4.25 ft to 4.75 ft.

Iteration 2—a larger bathroom

Again, we'll scale and print this model using the same settings from initial design and our first iteration. The file `ch7_iteration2.stl` inside MakerWare can be seen in the following screenshot:

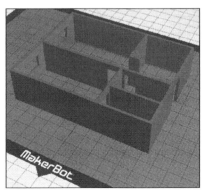

Iteration 2 in MakerWare

Now, we are happy with the flow and all the sizes; however, our 3D printed model is small, underwhelming, and hardly a show piece. What we'll do to fix this is increase the scale and print our model as an assembly. The increased scale will also help us later when we start adding more components to each of our rooms. Note that larger models will take longer to print.

We might have already been able to see these glaring issues just from looking at the floor plans on paper, and if that's the case, there is indeed no need to print the models. However, 3D printing can be utilized when we don't know the answer or when we are debating between multiple options. If we were to increase the size of our layout to say a 2, 3, or 4 bedroom home, we would have many more options. Sometimes, there may be multiple layouts whereby 3D printed models can help us conduct a side-by-side or a scenario comparison. We might even find ourselves in a situation where we are attached to more than one idea where by having a printed model, we can much more easily get input from clients or coworkers.

Third iteration

Now that we have done our first couple of iterations using a very simplistic model, we can now move on and increase the complexity. So, we can begin creating a presentation model.

We now have to ask ourselves, "How should we divide this floor plan? How large should each component be? How will we assemble all these components together?"

Division

Theoretically, we can divide the floor plan model; however, we choose and simply super glue all the pieces together to assemble our entire floor plan. However, if we are going to go through all the trouble of dividing our model, we should probably do so in a more intelligent way. What we should do is separate our assembly by individual rooms to keep our thoughts organized, and that way we don't mix and match bits of rooms.

 The simplest way to split rooms is to, on the Z plane, draw a square around the room you intend to keep. Then, extrude by cutting the rest of the model and save the file as a new part. Repeat the process until you have created parts for all the rooms.

Splitting the model in such a way will give us the files ch7_bathroom.stl, ch7_bedroom.stl, ch7_living_room.stl, ch7_closet.stl, and ch7_kitchen.stl. The following image is the file ch7_apt_assembly, which shows each of the individual parts/rooms using a different color:

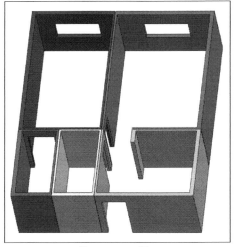

Room assembly

 Dividing the rooms through half the wall will ensure that your parting lines are less noticeable.

Size

Alright, so we have decided to divide the model by rooms, but now how big should these rooms be? We need to ensure that each room should be scaled by the same value in order to preserve their relative proportions. If we want an individual room to be printed as one model, our theoretical maximal room size is based on scaling the largest room to fit on the build platform. In the interest of preserving print time, let's make the largest room (living room) be about half the size of the build platform, which corresponds to a scale value of 0.02 (or 2 percent) which is a 1:50 total scale (double the size of the models from our previous iterations).

Assembly

Now that we've determined how we are splitting the model and how large each component will be, it's time to think about how we are going to assemble the final product and what amount of flexibility should we allow in our assembly.

Flexibility

The amount of flexibility in our model is left to our decision. We note that if we were to change the room locations or sizes using our model, the doorways would not line up and therefore, those pieces would be required to reprint. We could account for this by having our walls assemble to the floor. If we wanted to go a step further, we could even have our walls assemble to themselves, and then assemble to the floor. This way we could introduce a new doorway or window without having to reprint any pieces. The amount of flexibility is a difficult property to assign. Flexibility will save time when that component has to undergo numerous revisions, although unnecessary flexibility will just add unnecessary time and complexity to a project.

Before starting to complicate a project with flexibility, ask yourself, "Will this component change often?" and "How long would it take to make a flexible model of this versus how long would it take to redo for n number of changes?"

Our first two iterations were used to determine the room layout and room sizes; therefore, it's safe to say, at this point in time, that we are confident with our sizes and layouts. Because these components are not going to change, there is no purpose adding complexity to allow this functionality. Therefore, we can simply super glue all the rooms together to create our full presentation model. Let's print the following files using a **Low** resolution and super glue them together after each is done printing:

- ch7_bathroom.stl
- ch7_bedroom.stl
- ch7_living_room.stl
- ch7_closet.stl
- ch7_kitchen.stl

Upon assembling these components, we have our completed room layout for our single-story, one-bedroom, one-bathroom apartment. What we have printed is the barebones structure, but it looks a little empty. It's time we add some details.

Adding details

This is where we introduce the "wow" factor. Details are the most time-consuming part of this project and left to our discretion. In actuality, the amount of detail we can add to our model is endless, so what becomes important is the expected rate of return for the details we include. It's probably a poor use of time designing a pillow for the bed when the bathroom doesn't have a tub or the kitchen doesn't have a stove.

For this example, we're simply going to show the full detailing of a bathroom. The same process can be applied to detailing the remainder of the house. Let's add a toilet, sink and vanity, and bathtub/shower to create a fully detailed bathroom.

Toilet

Fortunately, we already found a suitable toilet model in *Chapter 6, The Community – Thingiverse and GrabCAD*. We'll use this model printed to a scale value of 50 percent. To print, we should use the **High** resolution settings. The following screenshot shows the toilet inside MakerWare. This ready-to-print file is labeled ch7_toilet.stl.

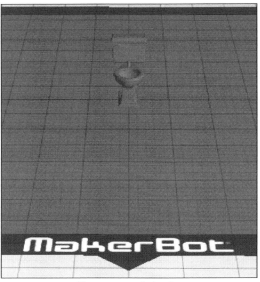

50 percent scaled toilet

Sink and vanity

We have already designed this object in *Chapter 6, The Community – Thingiverse and GrabCAD*. Let's just modify the scale to fit our application to a scale value of 30 percent. We should print this part using the **High** resolution as well, in order to minimize stepping in the sink. Let's also print this model in multicolor using Z Print, so our sink is of a different color from our vanity. This ready-to-print file is labeled ch7_sink_vanity_scaled.stl.

Bathtub/shower

Because of its simplicity, this component would be quicker to design ourselves rather than finding, editing, and scaling a model from GrabCAD or Thingiverse. The following image shows our model that is simplistic, but represents a shower well. Note that we could go into extensive detail while designing the shower, trying to model tiles or complex curvature, but this is not necessary for what we are trying to show. However, what we do need to make note of is tolerancing. We'll use a zero-clearance condition so that our shower stays firmly in place without the use of any glue. Our ready-to-print shower file is named `ch7_bathroom-shower.stl`.

Shower

Congratulations, we have successfully completed staging of the bathroom for our third iteration assembly floor plan, as seen in the following screenshot:

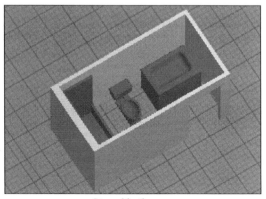

Staged bathroom

We choose to model our floor plan as an assembly in order to add more internal detail. If we were less concerned with internal details, we could potentially have stuck with our original scale, which would have halved the total print time.

Similar community examples

There are several models on Thingiverse of scaled houses. I invite you to check out these models and compare/contrast them with what we have just done. Note that we chose to model an apartment, thus not concerning ourselves with the exterior. Following are some links to models architectural model homes found on Thingiverse to give you an understanding of what's possible:

- The Puritan by MakerBot: http://www.thingiverse.com/thing:31644
- The Rodessa by MakerBot: http://www.thingiverse.com/thing:31645
- The Lorain by MakerBot: http://www.thingiverse.com/thing:31646
- The Chateau by MakerBot: http://www.thingiverse.com/thing:31643
- miniature version of a real existing house by BonsaiBrain: http://www.thingiverse.com/thing:5299
- the American Craftsman Bungalow Birdhouse by Erik JDurwoodll: http://www.thingiverse.com/thing:117080

Summary

This chapter focused on the practical example of creating the layout for a single-story one-bedroom, one-bathroom apartment. This room layout went through two revisions whereby 3D printing the model drove each revision. After these revisions were completed, we designed and printed a larger scale assembly of the most recent revision. We then focused on detailing the bathroom using models downloaded and edited from Thingiverse and GrabCAD, and also created it in our CAD package with appropriate tolerancing.

I hope you have enjoyed learning about applications of 3D printing in the field of architecture, and can now effectively apply these principles to your own outside projects and commercial assemblies.

Index

redesigning 47
specified supports 45
symmetry splitting 46
Z Print 46

S

second iteration 84, 85
Selective Laser Sintering. *See* SLS
shower, details 89, 90
sink, details 88
size, third iteration 86
SLA 6, 7
Slicer, advanced option 30
sliding fit. *See* clearance fit
SLS 7
software comparison
  modeling 15, 16
software packages
  Function 26, 27
  MakerWare 25-27
  ReplicatorG 25, 28
Solid Modeling 18
SolidWorks 17
specified supports 45
Speed | Speed while Travelling, advanced
    option 31
stereolithography. *See* SLA
Supports, option 30
symmetry splitting 46

T

Temperature | Build Plate, advanced option
    31
Temperature | Extruders, advanced option
    31
Thingiverse
  about 66
  maneuvering through 66-70
  URL 66

Thingiverse models
  Attribution license 70
  Attribution-NonCommercial license 71
  Attribution-ShareAlike license 71
  licensing 70
third iteration
  about 85
  assembly 86
  division 85, 86
  size 86
TinkerCAD 16
toilet model, details 88
tolerance 49
transition fit 51

V

vanity, details 88
veneer, design layout 60, 61
veneer, project scope 55, 56

W

wall thickness
  maintaining 20
warping
  avoiding 35, 36
while Extruding, advanced option 31
window, design layout 57, 58
window shape, design layout 58, 59
window size, design layout 58, 59
windows, project scope 55

Z

Z Pause 45
Z Print 46

Thank you for buying
3D Printing for Architects with MakerBot

About Packt Publishing

Packt, pronounced 'packed', published its first book "*Mastering phpMyAdmin for Effective MySQL Management*" in April 2004 and subsequently continued to specialize in publishing highly focused books on specific technologies and solutions.

Our books and publications share the experiences of your fellow IT professionals in adapting and customizing today's systems, applications, and frameworks. Our solution based books give you the knowledge and power to customize the software and technologies you're using to get the job done. Packt books are more specific and less general than the IT books you have seen in the past. Our unique business model allows us to bring you more focused information, giving you more of what you need to know, and less of what you don't.

Packt is a modern, yet unique publishing company, which focuses on producing quality, cutting-edge books for communities of developers, administrators, and newbies alike. For more information, please visit our website: www.packtpub.com.

Writing for Packt

We welcome all inquiries from people who are interested in authoring. Book proposals should be sent to author@packtpub.com. If your book idea is still at an early stage and you would like to discuss it first before writing a formal book proposal, contact us; one of our commissioning editors will get in touch with you.

We're not just looking for published authors; if you have strong technical skills but no writing experience, our experienced editors can help you develop a writing career, or simply get some additional reward for your expertise.

3D Printing Blueprints

ISBN: 978-1-84969-708-8   Paperback: 310 pages

Design successful models for home 3D printing, using a Makebot or other 3D printers

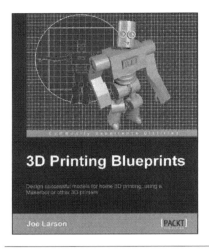

1. Design 3D models that will print successfully using Blender, a free 3D modelling program

2. Customize, edit, repair, and then share your creations on Makerbot's Thingiverse website

3. Easy-to-follow guide on 3D printing; learn to create a new model at the end of each chapter

KeyShot 3D Rendering

ISBN: 978-1-84969-482-7   Paperback: 124 pages

Showcase your 3D models and create hyperrealistic images with KeyShot in the fastest and most efficient way possible

1. Create professional quality images from your 3D models in just a few steps

2. Thorough overview of how to work and navigate in KeyShot

3. A step-by-step guide that quickly gets you started with creating realistic images

Please check **www.PacktPub.com** for information on our titles

Blender 2.6 Cycles: Materials and Textures Cookbook

ISBN: 978-1-78216-130-1   Paperback: 280 pages

Over 40 recipes to help you create stunning materials and textures using the Cycles rendering engine with Blender

1. Create naturalistic materials and textures, such as rock, snow, ice and fire, using Cycles

2. Learn Cycle's node-based material system

3. Get to grips with the powerful Cycles rendering engine

Instant Slic3r

ISBN: 978-1-78328-497-9   Paperback: 68 pages

Unravel the mysteries behind taking a virtual model and turning it into a physical object

1. Learn something new in an Instant! A short, fast, focused guide delivering immediate results

2. Use Slic3r to make your printed objects the best quality possible

3. Make Slic3r work for you, automating tasks and doing post processing on Slic3r output

4. The book is put together in a friendly and accessible manner to help walk you through the learning and how to use the software

Please check **www.PacktPub.com** for information on our titles

Made in the USA
San Bernardino, CA
13 January 2016